WHAT ARE OTHER PEOPLE SAYING

"TyAnn takes on a conversation that often only happens internally on the drive to and from the job as we sleepwalk through life. Bringing this taboo topic into the light offers us the opportunity to join her. The practical things "to do" will assist you with your self-discovery bringing a clarity and alignment to your life. I so recommend you give yourself the gift of this experience and allow the voice that is trying to get your attention some play time and discovery through these pages."

—**ALEXSYS THOMPSON**, AUTHOR OF *THE POWER OF A GRACEFUL LEADER*

"A Life Aligned is the much needed GPS for those trying to find meaning, purpose and joy in their lives. It is the definitive playbook that will guide the reader through their personal journey of conscious, intentional living. This is not a 'One and done' read. It is a systematic process to unlock your highest and best self that will be an invaluable reference throughout your life's journey."

—**JAYSON WOODWARD** WRITER, PRODUCER CHIEF COHERENCE/CONNECTIVITY, HIGHWAY 118 PRODUCTIONS, AUTHOR OF *BORDERLINE: A TRUE STORY OF COURAGE AND JUSTICE*

"Reading *A Life Aligned* like having your own personal leadership coach walking you through key questions to help you reset and reflect on your career and life. Ty's voice is the one you want guiding you through these decisions: authentic, relatable, and wise."

—**MEGAN W. GERHARDT, PH.D.**, FOUNDER & DIRECTOR OF THOUGHT LEADERSHIP, GENTELLIGENCE.ORG, PROFESSOR OF LEADERSHIP, MIAMI UNIVERSITY, AUTHOR, *GENTELLIGENCE: THE REVOLUTIONARY APPROACH TO LEADING AN INTERGENERATIONAL WORKFORCE*

"*A Life Aligned* is a compassionate, practical guide for anyone feeling burned out or disconnected. TyAnn combines personal stories with actionable insights, offering a roadmap to realign your life with your values and rediscover joy. A must-read for professionals seeking more meaning and energy."

—**BRANDON MILLER**, CO-FOUNDER & CEO, 34 STRONG,
AUTHOR OF *PLAY TO THEIR STRENGTHS* AND *INCREDIBLE PARENT*

"If you are a fellow PhD from the school of Suck It Up, Buttercup, drop what you're doing and read *A Life Aligned*. TyAnn shows us a joyful, motivating path to getting our energy back."

—**LISA CUMMINGS**, CEO OF LEAD THROUGH STRENGTHS

"This book is your friendly, thoughtful and helpful companion that will help you unpack everything you *think* drives you, and get really clear on what *actually* lights you up. TyAnn is the voice of reason you need right now, so you live life with intention, and pure joy."

—**KELLY IRVING**, BOOK COACH AND EDITOR,
FOUNDER OF THE EXPERT AUTHOR COMMUNITY

"A rare book definitely worth an in-depth exploration (maybe even twice). It hits many familiar and even unrecognized nerves, as well as delivers personal and professional insights, stories, analogies and wisdom that will stick with you forever."

—**CARTER MCCRARY**, GLOBAL C SUITE EXECUTIVE, FORTUNE 500 COMPANIES

"Reading *A Life Aligned* felt like being lovingly nudged by your straight-talking bestie—the one who tells it like it is, shares her own stumbles, and hands you a cuppa while asking, 'But how are you really?'

TyAnn's storytelling is equal parts heart and humor and the reflective questions she poses throughout will have you properly pausing and checking in with yourself to focus your energy on what REALLY matters.

This book isn't fluffy inspiration—it's practical—especially the mini scripts, reflective, with coaching gems that make change feel doable. Whether you're feeling stuck, burnt out, or just a bit off track, *A Life Aligned* offers a map back to yourself. Anyone not living their best life needs this book. And honestly, isn't that most of us at some point?"

—**CHARLOTTE BLAIR**, AUTHOR OF *CAREER UNSTUCK*,
AND COMMUNITY CONNECTOR

"*A Life Aligned* is a beautiful blend of wisdom, joy, wit, and encouragement—the kind of book that would have transformed my life two decades ago. TyAnn has a rare gift: she seamlessly steps into the dual role of cheerleader and sage, gently guiding you toward greater alignment. She was among the first to recognize the misalignment in my own life and encouraged me to take small but meaningful steps toward self-discovery. With a grounded mix of science, lived experience, and deep compassion, TyAnn invites us on a soulful, uplifting adventure—one that ultimately leads us back home to ourselves."

—**KYLA MARTIN**, FORMER FORTUNE 50 SPEECHWRITER TURNED CAREER COACH,
CO-HOST OF *TURN THE PAGE: DESIGN YOUR DREAM CAREER* PODCAST

A Life Aligned

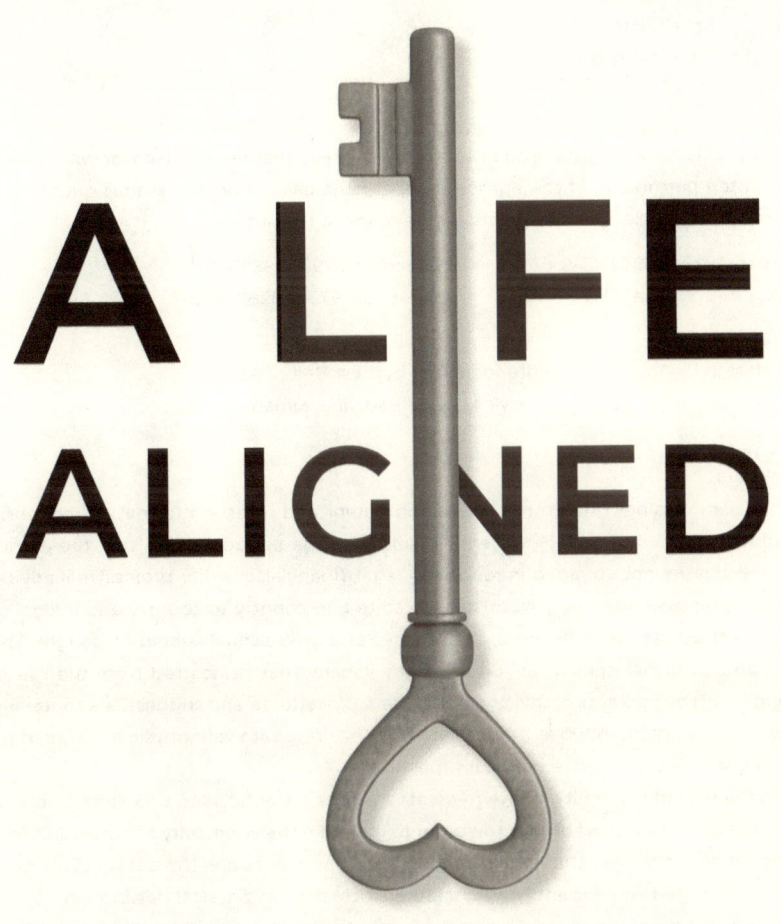

A LIFE ALIGNED

Keys to Transform
Your Work and Life

TYANN OSBORN

Disclaimers

This publication is designated to provide competent and reliable information regarding the subject matter covered. However, it is sold with the understanding that the author and publisher are not engaged in rendering legal, financial, or other professional advice. Laws and practices often vary from state to state and country to country and if legal or other expert assistance is required, the services of a professional should be sought. The author and publisher specifically disclaim any liability that is incurred from the use of application of the contents of this book. The ideas, procedures, and suggestions contained in this book are not intended as a substitute for consulting with your physician. All matters regarding your health require medical supervision.

To the best of my ability, I have re-created events, dates, locales, people and organizations from my memories of them. In order to maintain the anonymity of others, in some instances I have changed the names of individuals and places and the details of events. I have also changed some identifying characteristics, such as physical descriptions, occupations and places of residence. This book was written by memory, and mine is imperfect. I've done my best to be faithful to my experiences and, when possible, have consulted others who were also present during that time.

Gallup®, CliftonStrengths®, StrengthsFinder®, and the CliftonStrengths 34 Themes of Talent are trademarks of Gallup, Inc. All rights reserved. This publication also includes copyrighted content owned by Gallup, Inc. All Gallup intellectual property is used herein under a licensing agreement. The non-Gallup® information you are receiving has not been approved and is not sanctioned or endorsed by Gallup® in any way. Opinions, views, and interpretations of CliftonStrengths® are solely the beliefs of TyAnn Osborn, the author of this publication.

CONTENTS

CHAPTER ONE

How It All Began

ON A COMPLETELY average Saturday morning, I found myself in the frozen foods aisle at my neighborhood grocery store, searching for Cool Whip. I was exhausted from a long week of work, completely zoned out and operating on autopilot. That was my usual state outside of work.

I can't even remember why I needed the Cool Whip or why it seemed important. Maybe I was planning to eat it straight from the tub for dinner. As I stared at the rows of frozen containers, I glanced up and noticed a man pushing his cart toward me. At first, my brain didn't register anything. Then a faint, vague sense of familiarity flickered. He was with, who I assumed were, his wife and kids, and he was looking right at me.

"Crap," I thought, "what's this guy's name?"

Normally, I'm great with names. They're a huge part of my job. But as he approached, I drew a complete blank. He stopped his cart next to mine, my cart still closest to the freezer door I had left open, letting cold air spill out and raise goosebumps on my arms.

"Hey, Ty, remember me?" he asked.

Dang it. The absolute worst scenario when you don't remember someone, right? I frantically searched my memory. Did we work together? Was he the mechanic from the oil change place I'd been to recently? Was he a cousin? (Not a stretch—I'd forgotten a cousin's name at the store not long ago.) But nothing. My mind was a foggy void.

"Hey, you," I stammered. It was painfully obvious to everyone that I had no idea who he was. Politely, he introduced me to his wife and kids. "Nice to meet you," I replied automatically. But then he said something that would haunt me for years.

"My name is Brian," he paused, almost dramatically. "You fired me two weeks ago."

In that instant, my heart stopped. My brain spun like the prize wheel on *The Price is Right*. What had I been doing two weeks ago? Firing people, as usual. But how many? And who? Unlike the prize wheel, my mind didn't land on anything. I couldn't remember.

Then it hit me, like the Roadrunner crushed under a pile of Acme bricks. The weight was crushing, my breath caught in my throat.

I had fired so many people that I didn't even remember him.

Beyond that vague recognition, there was nothing—just fog. Nothing about his termination stood out, nothing about his notification meeting was any different from the countless others I'd conducted. I must have looked like a fish gasping for air. I don't know how long I stood there before I managed to speak again. To this day, I can't remember what I said, but I know it was a weak, mumbled response that did nothing to make the situation better.

I wish I could tell you I did something compassionate, like paying for his groceries. But I didn't. I was numb. My brain had shut down.

I didn't get anything else on my list—not even the Cool Whip. I somehow made it to the checkout, paid for my groceries without a second thought about my bank balance and walked back to my car. The car I didn't worry about making payments on. To the house I could easily afford. My job—firing people—was secure. That was the one constant.

Sitting in the driver's seat, I broke down. I cried for Brian and his family. I cried for all the people whose final memory of the company was me, delivering the bad news. I cried for the role I played, the hatchet person.

As I sat there in the parking lot, I began taking stock of my life. How had I ended up here? I was often sick. I had few real friends—most were just work acquaintances. I didn't even know my neighbors. I had no hobbies. Sure, I was educated, but it didn't take an MBA to fire people. I had become an empty shell, sleepwalking through life.

MY ORIGIN STORY

I come from Generation X, raised by parents who were part of the tail end of the Traditionalist generation—those born just before the Boomers around World War II, with parents who had lived through the Great Depression. For them, work wasn't about passion or fulfillment; it was about survival and getting the job done. If I had called either my mom or dad for advice on work, they wouldn't have had much to offer beyond "keep going and tough it out." Not because they didn't care, but because that's how they had been taught to navigate life.

My mom, a high school teacher, never would have considered leaving a job just because she didn't like it. Women of her generation had limited career choices—she picked teaching over nursing simply because she hated blood. My dad, a police officer, went straight from farming to Vietnam, and emerged with an unshakeable work ethic. I have no memory of him ever relaxing unless it involved sitting on a tractor. He was raised to believe, in the words of Dr. James Hollis, to "suit up, show up and shut up." Vulnerability wasn't part of the equation for his generation. Concepts like mindfulness, emotional awareness and personal fulfillment would only become mainstream much later.

Growing up, I watched both of my parents go to work every day, often burned out and exhausted, until they retired in poor health. My father struggled so much with the idea of retirement that he went back to work as a consultant. It was like he couldn't fathom a life that wasn't built around constant busyness, even though his body was telling him otherwise. "Heading out to the salt mines" was a common expression in our household, referencing the grueling nature of their jobs, and it was understood that work was something you endured, not something you enjoyed.

This was the world I grew up in, and like many in my generation, I absorbed those lessons. It wasn't about finding joy or purpose in your work—it was about figuring things out on your own and getting by. That mindset shaped me, but it also left me feeling unfulfilled, wondering if there was more to life than just putting in time. Eventually, that realization became the catalyst for rethinking my own path.

MY EPIPHANY

When that moment in the grocery store happened, I thought I was the only person on the planet feeling what I was feeling—sadness, regret, confusion, uncertainty, even anger. It was incredibly isolating to believe no one else was experiencing that blend of emotions, and it left me more lonely than I already was. I didn't think anyone else would understand and it certainly didn't feel "safe" to reach out to anyone and talk about it. Besides, who would really get it? I was making a good income at a prestigious company with a well-known brand. I could already hear the chorus in my head: "These must be first-world problems."

I couldn't figure out how I had gone from a bright-eyed college graduate to the hatchet person. Where had I gone wrong?

On top of all that, I thought this was just how work was supposed to be. You know, it sucks, but you suck it up and do it—hence the old "it's called work for a reason!" mantra. Rinse and repeat for 40 years until retirement. So, even though I knew I had somehow gotten stuck doing something I definitely didn't love, I also felt like something was wrong with *me* because I couldn't just get with the program. Surely other people weren't having these kinds of existential crises, right? It didn't seem that way. My company was filled with over-achievers desperate to get ahead. So, it had to be just me.

Over time however, I began to realize it wasn't just me. Slowly, through conversations with friends and clients, I started paying attention to what they were saying, to what they were feeling. At first, it was subtle—offhand remarks about stress or feeling disconnected from their work. But as I listened more closely, I heard the same undertones of dissatisfaction, the same weariness I felt. They, too, were stuck in roles that didn't inspire them, doing things that drained them rather than fueled them. It wasn't just me after all.

What surprised me most was how many of them, from different industries and backgrounds, shared this same sense of being trapped in something they didn't love. Many of them were high achievers, successful on the surface, yet they privately confessed feeling unfulfilled, as if they were simply going through the motions. These conversations slowly peeled away the isolation I had felt. I wasn't alone in this existential struggle. It wasn't a personal failure. It was a shared experience, one that many people—just like me—had been quietly battling for years.

That realization—that I wasn't alone in feeling trapped in work that drained me—was a turning point. It was no longer just about surviving the day-to-day grind; it became about taking action. I began to spend time reflecting on what truly mattered to me. What kind of work would make me feel fulfilled? What did I value at my core? These questions weren't easy to answer at first. They required me to dig deep, to strip away the layers of expectation and pressure I had placed on myself over the years. But slowly, the fog lifted, and I began to see a clearer picture of what I wanted my life to look like.

It wasn't just about escaping the job I was in; it was about transforming my entire professional life into something that aligned with my values and my purpose. I started mapping out the changes I needed to make—small steps at first. I sought out opportunities that excited me, that allowed me to create, to connect with others, and to make a meaningful impact. I re-evaluated my priorities, letting go of roles and tasks that didn't serve my long-term goals, and re-directed my focus toward projects that aligned with who I was at my core.

This wasn't an overnight shift, but with every new choice, I felt a growing sense of alignment between what I did and who I wanted to be. The more I leaned into this process, the more energy and passion I found for my work. I realized that by making intentional choices to live and work in alignment with my values, I could build a career that didn't drain me, but instead fueled me. And that made all the difference.

WHAT ABOUT YOU?

Let's do a quick feelings check. Take a moment and ask yourself:

- Do you feel unfulfilled, disenchanted, or stuck in your work or life?
- Have you reached a level of success, whether it's a degree, a job title, a certain income, or a leadership role, only to realize it's not what you thought it would be?
- Do you feel like you've worked hard to climb a ladder, as Zig Zigler says, only to find it's leaning against the wrong wall?
- Are you unsure how to break free from this feeling of being stuck or how to make your life better?
- Do you wonder how to rediscover your joy, talents, or purpose?
- Are you struggling to align your gifts or passions with your ability to make a living?

If you answered "yes" to any of these questions, you're not alone, and you're in the right place.

Let's take a moment to reflect on your current work situation and its effect on you. Think about these areas of your work life and your overall satisfaction. Check the appropriate box:

	Very happy	Somewhat satisfied	Meh	Somewhat dissatisfied	Very unhappy
Job Title					
Work Responsibilities					
Direct Manager					
Employer					
Opportunities for advancement					
Opportunities for continued learning and development					

What insights did you discover by doing that reflection exercise? Have you identified places where you feel dissatisfied, weary, depressed, or stuck?

I've been there. I've been exactly where you are. And I'm here to tell you that there is another way. A different way. A better way. I don't want you to stay stuck, and I care because I've discovered my purpose: to help others get their lives in alignment.

That's the point of this book. Through our time together, I will help you uncover your true purpose, get in alignment with your values and your strengths, and take the steps necessary to transform your life into one that feels vibrant, fulfilling, and full of passionate purpose.

If I can go from being the company hatchet person, crying in a parking lot, to the owner of a thriving business where we help others find their worth and joy, then you can make that change too. I promise. But it doesn't happen overnight, and it doesn't happen without intentional thought and effort.

THE OBJECTIONS

I can already hear some of you pushing back, saying to yourself, "Well yeah, Ty, that's great, but I could never make a change because of my unique situation." You might be thinking something like:

- I have kids or other dependent family to worry about.
- I'm too old or too established in my career already.

- I'm the breadwinner and we can't afford to lose our income or health insurance.
- I have a partner who isn't supportive—or no partner to rely on at all.
- I've got chronic medical issues.
- I have aging parents to care for.
- I don't have the right education or experience to do something else.

Here's the truth: You're going to get older no matter what you start—or don't start—right now. In 10 years, we will all be 10 years older. Time is the great equalizer in life. The question is, would you rather spend those 10 years feeling the way you do now? If so, keep on going as you are. But if not, consider that there may be a different way to approach life, one that could lead to a different, better result.

By the way, I also have children in a blended family, I'm over 50 and I was considered an expert in my previous field when I left to start my own company. I've gone through stretches of life on my own, as well as periods spent with someone who offered little to no genuine support. I've dealt with a grab bag of medical issues, have parents and in-laws in their late seventies with serious health problems—some in assisted living—and more. One thing I've learned along the way is that everyone is going through something.

I'm sharing my story because I get it. I've faced many of the same challenges. But you need to hear this: you have amazing gifts to share with the world. I promise—you do. I know this to the core of my being. That is why you are here. And if you're stuck in those depressive feelings there's no way you're sharing the best of you. The best of you is what you, and the rest of the world, deserve.

So, how do you show up as your best, most authentic, version of yourself? You come into alignment with who you truly are and then take steps to create a life that aligns with that as well.

WHAT IS ALIGNMENT?

Alignment is the state of being in harmony with your authentic self—your values, passions, strengths and purpose. It's when your actions, decisions and priorities reflect who you truly are at your core. Alignment isn't about perfection or constant certainty; it's about living intentionally, making choices that feel right for you and creating a life that energizes and fulfills you rather than drains and confines you.

WHY DOES ALIGNMENT MATTER?

When you're aligned with your authentic self, life feels more meaningful and purposeful. You're able to focus your energy on what truly matters to you, rather than conforming to external expectations or societal pressures. Alignment brings clarity, reduces inner conflict and allows you to experience joy, resilience and connection in deeper, more genuine ways. It's the foundation for a life that feels vibrant and whole.

THE COST OF BEING OUT OF ALIGNMENT

When you're out of alignment, life often feels heavy, disconnected or exhausting. You may feel stuck in roles or routines that don't serve you, chasing goals that don't fulfill you. Signs of being out of alignment include:

- **Chronic dissatisfaction**: You feel drained, disenchanted, or unmotivated.
- **Inner conflict**: Decisions feel forced, and your actions clash with your values.
- **Stress and burnout**: You're constantly overextended, with little energy or passion left for what you enjoy.
- **Loss of identity**: You may struggle to recognize who you are or what truly makes you happy.

The cost of misalignment is high—leading to physical, emotional and mental exhaustion, and a life that feels like it's slipping away without purpose or fulfillment.

THE BENEFITS OF LIVING IN ALIGNMENT

Living in alignment is liberating and transformative. When your life reflects your authentic self, you experience:

- **Clarity and focus:** Decisions become easier because they align with your core values.
- **Energy and passion:** Work and relationships feel meaningful and enriching, not depleting.
- **Inner peace**: You're not in constant conflict with yourself or others; you feel balanced and grounded.
- **Confidence and fulfillment**: You trust your path and embrace your unique gifts, knowing you're contributing to the world in a way that matters.
- **Resilience:** Life's challenges are easier to navigate because you're living with purpose and authenticity.

ALIGNMENT IN PRACTICE

Alignment doesn't mean every day is perfect or that challenges disappear. It means knowing who you are, what you stand for and making decisions that honor that. When you're in alignment, your work, relationships and habits feel like natural extensions of your true self, creating a life that fuels you rather than drains you. This state of harmony allows you to experience life with clarity, confidence, and joy.

TAKE THE FIRST STEP

There are specific changes you can start making today that will dramatically shift the trajectory of your life. I encourage you to join me in exploring the stories and activities in this book, designed to help you uncover your unique gifts and possibilities, and map out a plan for what's next.

Ask yourself: *What will your life look like in a year if you change nothing and continue on as you have been?* You'll either stay the same or feel even worse. But if you choose to be brave and make the decision to change, you'll be amazed at where the journey can take you. Choose courage.

REFLECTION INSTRUCTIONS FOR ALL ACTIVITIES:

1. FIND A QUIET PLACE TO REFLECT.

This isn't something to do in the middle of a busy living room, with the TV on or Alexa reminding you to reorder refrigerator filters. Sometimes I go sit in my car. You need a space where you can escape the noise of everyday life. That constant noise is what often drowns out the whispers of clarity.

2. CLOSE YOUR EYES AND TAKE A DEEP BREATH.

Focus on the air filling your lungs and slowly leaving your nose and mouth. Repeat this three times to get centered and bring blood flow to your brain.

3. HAVE A NOTEBOOK AND PEN READY TO JOT DOWN THOUGHTS, OR USE THE WHITE SPACE IN THIS BOOK.

Analog tools work best for this kind of reflection and studies show that writing by hand helps ideas "stick" in your brain better than digital notes. I like to use a dedicated notebook and my favorite pen. Make this part fun for you—use colors, stickers, or whatever makes you smile! Personally, I use a Kate Spade notebook with a cheeky quip on the cover because it brightens my day.

ALIGNMENT QUIZ

Let's take a look at your current level of alignment. Don't worry—it isn't difficult or intended to cause more stress! We are just getting a quick starting baseline.

Read the statements below and think about how often you've felt this way in the past few months. Then put a check mark in the corresponding box.

Note that this is not a diagnostic tool for mental health. That determination can only be made by a mental health profes-sional. Please seek one out if you are concerned.

	Always	Often	Sometimes	Rarely	Never
I feel that my life is very rewarding.					
I can see the goodness in myself.					
I can see the goodness in those around me.					
I am surrounded by positive people.					
I understand my talents and gifts.					
I feel hopeful about the future.					
I feel pleasure daily.					
I can name specific moments of joy in my life.					
I understand my purpose in life.					

	Always	Often	Sometimes	Rarely	Never
I have hobbies and activities outside of work.					
I have the right amount of energy.					
I reach out for help and support when I need it.					
TOTAL					

Now count the number of check marks in each column and put that in the Total box for that column.

If most of your check marks are in the "Always" and "Often" columns, you likely have a good understanding of your motivations and feel pretty aligned with your purpose. That's great! Let's explore how you got here and how to keep you on this path.

If most of your check marks fall into the "Sometimes" column, you might have some room for improvement. While certain areas of your life may be working well, others could benefit from positive changes. Let's keep what is working and identify any areas for improvement so we can tweak those.

If most of your check marks are in the "Rarely" or "Never" columns, it's a sign that you need change. Without some adjustments, you may be on track for burnout or are already there. Let's create a plan for your success.

This book is designed as a journey. You can read it straight through or skip to the chapters that are most relevant to you. Each chapter includes reflection activities and questions. I encourage you to take the time to complete them, as they will form the foundation of your alignment plan. You can also access the exercises as a fillable PDF download at www.alifealignedbook.com.

Together, we're going to identify the reasons behind your professional dissatisfaction or despair, unlock the passion and purpose within you and then equip you to be able to create a life that aligns with who you truly are.

The truth is that our generation wasn't taught that we should pursue our individual passions, unless that passion led straight to an established, well-paying job. We weren't told that what we had to offer was precious and valuable. Instead, we learned that we had to have our lifelong occupation figured out by the time we graduated from high school and that once we set our feet on a career path, we kept plugging away at that road for decades until one day we could finally retire.

In this book, I want to help you give yourself permission to embrace a new paradigm—one where you're no longer bound by the old idea that you must pick a career straight out of school and stick with it until retirement, even if it no longer aligns with your passions. Today, we have more options. It's okay to question your path, lean into uncomfortable feelings and explore where they're coming from rather than pushing them aside. By doing this, you can make changes—big or small—that will bring your life into better alignment with who you are and what you truly want.

My goal is to empower you to feel confident and brave enough to take those steps. You have the permission to dream, to take risks, and to nurture the life you've always wanted. This isn't about making reckless decisions, but about thoughtfully taking action that moves you closer to a life filled with purpose and joy. As you move through these pages, I hope you not only dream big but also feel inspired to take practical steps toward making those dreams a reality. 🔑

CHAPTER TWO

Identify the Season You're In

TO PARAPHRASE JULIE Andrews in *The Sound of Music*: the beginning is a very good place to start. So, let's start with a little thought experiment. Imagine walking into a classroom full of 9-year-old kids. You introduce yourself, smile and ask, "Who here has a talent? Who's good at something?" What happens next?

If you've ever tried this, you know what's coming. Chaos—in the best way. Hands shoot up instantly. Sometimes both hands. Kids squirm in their seats, bouncing like popcorn. They can't wait to be called on, shouting, "Ooh, pick me! Pick me!"

And their answers? Unfiltered, uninhibited and endlessly entertaining. I've heard it all: video games, skateboarding, singing, drawing, monkey bars, making macaroni and cheese, burping the alphabet, armpit farts—you name it. Kids own their talents with pride, no matter how quirky or unconventional.

They're not just good at something—they *know* they're good at it and they can't wait to tell you.

Now let's flip the script. Picture a boardroom instead of a classroom. I walk in, smile and ask the exact same question: "Who here has a talent? Who's good at something?" What happens?

Silence. People suddenly become very interested in their shoes. No hands go up. No one is shouting, "Pick me!" It's as if I've just asked them to admit a crime. When adults finally do respond, it's hesitant, self-deprecating and often wrapped in qualifiers like, "Well, I used to be good at..." or "I mean, I'm okay at..."

Here's what's fascinating: never—not once—has a child answered my question with, "Well, I'm not *that* good," or "Someone else is better than me," or "I can't make a living doing that." But adults? Those are the exact responses I hear all the time—if they're willing to answer at all.

What happened between childhood and adulthood? Why did so many of us stop raising our hands? And more importantly, how do we get back to that joyful, unfiltered confidence? That's what we're going to explore in this chapter. It starts by identifying the season you're in—and rediscovering what makes you come alive. Let's dig in.

SO WHAT HAPPENED?

What happens between our 9-year-old self and our adult self that causes this shift? At what point do our hands go from waving enthusiastically in the air to hanging quietly at our sides? It's not an overnight transformation but a gradual one, shaped by the messages we receive from teachers, parents, other adults, society, and media. At 9 it's adorable to dream of becoming a rock star or President, but by 13 those same dreams are met with skepticism or outright dismissal. The eye rolls begin, and with them come the first cracks in our confidence.

These messages creep in slowly, subtly and sometimes directly. They sound like, "You can't make a living at that," or "You need to become an accountant/doctor/engineer to get ahead." Maybe it's, "You're not that good at piano/drawing/singing, so you should quit," or "Acting isn't a real job." Sometimes, it's an anecdote about failure: "Yeah, your Uncle Mark wanted to be an artist too, and now he lives in a van and can't hold down a real job." Other times it's a more insidious limitation, like, "Boys don't do that job," or "That field isn't for people like us." These statements build up over time, working like water over rock—slowly eroding our joyful, unfiltered confidence.

The Gallup organization studies this phenomenon and their research shows a precipitous drop in student engagement from a high of 76% in elementary, to 61% in middle school, to a low of 44% in high school. According to Gallup, "the drop in student engagement for each year students are in school is our monumental, collective national failure."[1]

By the time we reach adulthood, many of us have fully internalized these messages, often without even realizing it. We stop dreaming as boldly, we start censoring our ambitions and we downplay our talents for fear of being judged or ridiculed. It's no wonder so many adults hesitate to call themselves "good" at anything or find joy in their unique gifts. We've spent years absorbing societal expectations about what's "realistic," "practical" or "worthy"—and those ideas rarely leave room for unabashed self-belief. These feelings aren't just relegated to our home lives, they also spill over into work. Our entire day is colored by how we feel about ourselves.

Gallup further reports that by the time young adults enter the workforce, engagement levels are down to 33%. That means that if you line up with your co-workers, about 7 out of 10 of you don't like your jobs. You might be phoning it in at best, or actively acting out your unhappiness at worst. I know I have. But that's not ok. Let that feeling be an indicator, a light on your car dashboard so to speak, that something needs to change.

The result? We squash our butterflies—the little sparks of joy and wonder that make us unique. Our hands stay at our sides, not because we lack talent, but because we've been conditioned to believe it doesn't matter. But here's the thing:

---

1. Gallup. (2013, January 7). The school cliff: Student engagement drops with each school year. Retrieved from https://news.gallup.com/opinion/gallup/170525/school-cliff-student-engagement-drops-school-year.aspx

it *does* matter. Those butterflies, those sparks, are still inside you, waiting to be nurtured and set free. The first step is recognizing the season you're in and giving yourself permission to reclaim the joy you once felt.

LET'S TALK ABOUT SEASONS

Life moves in seasons, just like nature. Some seasons are vibrant and flourishing—like summer, when opportunities feel endless and energy abounds. Others are quiet and introspective, like winter, when everything feels still, and progress seems invisible under a blanket of snow. And just like the natural seasons every season of life has a purpose. Recognizing which one you're in is the first step toward understanding your baseline and uncovering the opportunities that season offers. It's also the first step toward reigniting your creative spark and reclaiming your joy and confidence.

Think of it this way: If you're in spring, you're planting seeds. Maybe you're starting a new project, relationship or chapter of life. It's a time of growth and possibility. Summer is where you see the fruits of your labor begin to bloom—this is a season of abundance and creativity, a time to lean into your talents and confidence. Fall can bring change, a chance to harvest the rewards of your efforts while also letting go of things that no longer serve you. And winter? Winter isn't a time to panic or despair. It's a season for rest, reflection and preparation for what's next. The ground may look barren, but underneath, the soil is replenishing itself, quietly making space for growth to begin again.

Identifying your current season isn't just about naming it—it's about using it as a baseline to reconnect with yourself. Maybe you've been stuck in the quiet of winter, unsure how to move forward, or maybe you're in the middle of a vibrant summer but still feel disconnected from joy and creativity. Wherever you are, understanding your season helps you see the unique opportunities it offers and how you can start to realign with what lights you up.

When you know your season, you can work with its rhythm instead of against it. You can stop comparing yourself to someone else's summer and start focusing on how to nurture your own creative spark. You can use that awareness to take meaningful steps toward reclaiming your confidence, rediscovering your joy and leaning into the purpose that's already waiting for you. Let's figure out which season you're in and how to use it to build the life you want.

YOU KEEP USING THAT WORD

I know, I know... I keep focusing on "joy," a concept that often doesn't feel very adult or practical in our current culture. It certainly doesn't get the time and energy that words like "productivity" and "paying the bills" receive. However, joy isn't just a luxury—it's essential. It's easy to think of joy as the icing on the cake of life, something you get to experience only after all the "important" things are done. But the truth is, joy is one of the most important things. It's the fuel that powers your mental health, creativity and overall alignment. Without it, even the most well-constructed life can feel empty and unfulfilling.

When joy is present, it acts like a supercharger for your brain and body. Studies show that experiencing joy reduces stress, improves focus and increases resilience. Think about the last time you felt truly joyful—didn't it make everything feel a little easier, even the hard stuff? Joy opens the door to possibilities. It helps you see opportunities where before there were only obstacles. It's what makes you adaptable, innovative and able to bounce back when life throws you a curveball.

Joy also plays a critical role in creativity. When you're joyful, your mind is more open and curious. You're more willing to take risks, explore new ideas and think outside the box. Joy quiets the inner critic—the voice that tells you you're not good enough or that your ideas are silly—and makes room for inspiration to flow. That's why aligning your life with what brings you joy isn't just about feeling good; it's about unlocking your ability to create, problem-solve and grow.

Beyond that, joy is what keeps you connected to yourself. It's a reminder of who you are and what truly matters to you. When you prioritize joy, you're prioritizing alignment—living a life that reflects your values, talents and passions. Without it you're more likely to feel disconnected, stuck or out of sync with the life you're trying to build.

So, let's stop treating joy as an afterthought and start recognizing it as the foundation for a life that feels vibrant and fulfilling. By leaning into the things that ignite joy, you're not just enhancing your mental health and creativity—you're also setting the stage for a life that feels deeply aligned with who you are. Because when joy leads, everything else starts to fall into place.

So, what ignites joy for you? Let's figure it out. We'll do this in 4 steps.

STEP 1: ESTABLISH YOUR BASELINE

Before you can figure out where you're going, you need to know where you are. It's time to establish your baseline—an honest assessment of your emotional, mental and physical state. Think of this as taking the pulse of your life right now. No judgment, no pressure—just curiosity and awareness.

Let's start by grounding ourselves in the idea of seasons. If your life were a season right now, which one would it be? Winter, spring, summer or fall? Take a moment to reflect on this. Are you in a winter—feeling like you're in a holding pattern, needing rest or clarity? Maybe it's spring—a time of fresh starts and new ideas. Summer might mean you're thriving, creating and full of energy, while fall could be a season of change and letting go of what no longer serves you.

Complete this sentence:

"Right now, my life feels like _____
because _____."

This simple exercise can help you begin to articulate where you are and why. For example:

- "Right now, my life feels like winter because I've been feeling tired and disconnected, like I need time to rest and reflect."
- "Right now, my life feels like summer because I'm juggling a lot of creative projects and while it's exciting, it's also overwhelming."

REFLECT ON THESE AREAS OF YOUR LIFE

Once you've identified your season, let's go a little deeper.
Consider these three areas of your life:

1. EMOTIONAL STATE

How are you feeling on a day-to-day basis? Are you energized,
hopeful and inspired? Or do you feel drained, frustrated or
stuck?

    Write this down:

"Emotionally, I feel _____
because _____**."**

2. MENTAL STATE

What's the quality of your thoughts right now? Are you
focused, motivated and curious? Or are you struggling with
overthinking, negativity, or feeling directionless?

    Write this down:

"Mentally, I feel _____
because _____**."**

3. PHYSICAL STATE

How is your body feeling? Do you have energy, strength and a sense of well-being? Or are you dealing with fatigue, stress or neglecting your physical needs?

Write this down:

"Physically, I feel _____

because _____**."**

BRINGING IT ALL TOGETHER

Now, look at what you've written. Does it paint a clear picture of the season you're in? Maybe your emotional and mental states feel like fall—ready for change—but your physical state is stuck in winter, needing rest and care. This isn't about per- fection or alignment just yet—it's about awareness.

TAKING STOCK

Take a moment to jot down one word or phrase that captures your overall baseline. Then ask yourself:

- What about this season feels challenging?
- What about this season feels full of possibility?

For example:

"I'm in winter, and it feels hard because I don't know how to move forward, but it also feels full of possibility because I have time to reflect and recharge."

This baseline isn't a permanent record report card for anyone else's eyes—it's a starting point just for you. Once you know where you're starting from, you can begin to make choices that move you toward the creative spark, joy and confidence you want to reclaim.

Let's use this awareness as fuel for what comes next: identifying what brings you joy and learning how to lean into it.

STEP 2: IDENTIFY WHAT BRINGS YOU JOY

Here's the truth: our likes often point to our talents and our talents hold the key to crafting a life that feels aligned with who we are. The problem is, somewhere along the way, many of us lose touch with the things that bring us joy. That joyful, unfiltered confidence we had as kids gets drowned out by responsibilities, expectations and the negative chatter in our own heads. But here's the good news—you haven't lost it completely. It's still there, waiting for you to tap back in.

HEY, WAIT A MINUTE

You might be thinking, *I didn't have a good childhood. I didn't like anything as a kid. I can't remember back that far. What does this have to do with aligning my life now?* And that's valid. Everyone has challenges in childhood—some more than others. I'm not asking you to sugarcoat your past or invent memories that weren't there. What I'm asking is this: Can you take a moment to search for even the smallest spark of positivity from that time?

I've spoken to many people from all walks of life, and I've found that even in the hardest circumstances, children still experience moments of joy. It might not be something huge or obvious, but it's there—a game they loved to play, a hobby that caught their interest or even a simple activity that brought comfort. These sparks, no matter how small, can reveal something about who you are at your core. Creative abilities, artistic talents, athletic potential and other gifts often emerge early, even if they weren't nurtured or recognized at the time.

So, take a deep breath and let yourself mentally travel back. What small moments brought light to your childhood? What did you gravitate toward, even if it was fleeting? These moments matter because they offer clues to your unique talents and joys. They're not about living in the past—they're about using your past to guide your present and shape a future that feels more aligned with who you truly are.

READY? HERE WE GO

Let's start by quieting that mind chatter and reconnecting with the wisdom of your 9-year-old self. You know, the version of you who didn't overthink everything, who simply *liked* things because they were fun, exciting or interesting. The version of you who didn't worry if liking something made sense or if you were "good enough" at it.

Close your eyes for a moment and take yourself back to being 9. Picture yourself in your childhood bedroom or your favorite spot to play. What did you love to do? What made you lose track of time? What were you naturally drawn to?

REFLECTION ACTIVITY:
RECONNECTING WITH JOY

Now, let's put this into action.

1. Grab your journal (or use the space in this book) and your favorite pen.

2. Set a timer for **2 minutes.**

3. Write down **everything** you like and think you're good at. No editing, no filtering. Don't worry if it's "you at work" or "you at home." Just write. If you like singing in the shower, it goes on the list. If you're great at remembering birthdays, write that down too.

4. Keep going until the timer runs out.

5. When you're done, count the number of things you wrote down.

WHAT DID YOU DISCOVER?

In my workshops I ask people to share their numbers. Most people list around 7 things, and the record so far is 42. What's your number?

Now, think about the process of making your list. Did you find it easy? Were you still writing when the timer went off, or did you start strong and then stall? Maybe you struggled to get started at all. Did those butterfly-squashing thoughts creep in—"You're not really that good," or "That's not a thing"?

Take a closer look at your list. What kinds of things did you write down? Can you spot any patterns? Are they creative activities like cooking, crafting or playing music? Maybe they're relationship-oriented, like being a good listener or connecting with people. Are there connections to specific places, tools or processes you enjoy?

Even if the connections aren't obvious yet, that's okay. Sometimes patterns take time to emerge. Just know that your list is a window into the things that bring you joy and where your talents might naturally lie.

MY 9-YEAR-OLD WISDOM

Let me share an example from my own life. As a kid, I loved reading and learning about how things were made. I vividly remember an episode of *Mr. Rogers' Neighborhood* where he showed a video about how zippers were made in a factory. I was absolutely captivated! To this day, if I had the chance to tour a zipper factory, I'd jump at it (and I'd probably be the oldest kid on the field trip).

I also loved reading books in a series, like *Nancy Drew*. I enjoyed organizing those books on my shelf, keeping them in perfect order. That love of stories and my appreciation for a well-organized bookshelf has stayed with me into adulthood. They're small things, but they point to enduring passions: my love of storytelling and my need for order and structure.

YOUR JOY, YOUR TALENTS

The things you liked as a kid aren't random. They're clues—breadcrumbs leading you back to your talents and passions. When you rediscover what lights you up, you can start to reconnect with your confidence, creativity and joy.

Let your list be your guide. What stands out to you? What patterns are emerging? And most importantly, how can you start making space for those things in your life right now? Let's keep exploring. You're already on your way.

STEP 3: PERMISSION TO FEEL PLEASURE

Here's the thing: joy and pleasure often get tangled up with guilt. Somewhere along the way, many of us internalized the idea that if something feels good, it must be unproductive, indulgent or selfish. We're taught to prioritize hard work, responsibility and achievement—and while those are valuable, they often come at the expense of the simple pleasures that make life meaningful.

How often have you stopped yourself from doing something you love because you felt you didn't "deserve" it? Maybe you've said, "I don't have time for that right now," or "I'll enjoy myself later, once I've finished this task, this project, this goal." But here's the catch: there's always another task, another project, another goal. If you keep postponing joy, you risk waking up one day and realizing it's no longer a part of your life.

Let me tell you a story. I once met someone who loved painting. It brought her joy, calmed her mind and made her feel alive. But she stopped because she didn't think she was "good enough" to justify spending time on it. She told herself that if it didn't lead to a side hustle or an Instagram-worthy masterpiece, it wasn't worth it. The result? She felt more disconnected and stressed than ever. It wasn't until she gave herself permission to paint *just because*—with no pressure, no expectations—that she began to rediscover her spark.

This struggle isn't uncommon. Societal and personal barriers often whisper (or shout) that pleasure is frivolous or undeserved. But here's the truth: joy and pleasure are not rewards for hard work. **They are necessities for a balanced, fulfilling life**. You don't have to justify what lights you up. Whether it's painting, reading, gardening, or simply enjoying a quiet cup of coffee, these moments matter. They fuel your creativity, replenish your energy and remind you of who you are.

HOW ABOUT YOU?

Take a moment to reflect: **What brings you guilt-free pleasure?** If nothing comes to mind right away, don't panic. Sometimes we get so caught up in life that we forget what makes us happy. Think small—maybe it's walking outside, cooking your favorite meal, dancing in the kitchen or watching a favorite show. For me, I still enjoy reading and getting lost in new stories. While I don't read as much as I'd like, it is still something that brings me joy and I look forward to.

If you're still drawing a blank, ask yourself: **What small things could I explore that might bring me joy?** Give yourself permission to try something new or revisit an old favorite. Remember, it's not about perfection or productivity—it's about letting yourself enjoy the moment, guilt-free. Maybe this is a great time to explore that cooking class you heard about, sourdough bread making, anyone?

Pleasure isn't a luxury, it's a lifeline. It's time to stop waiting for permission and start giving it to yourself. The joy you allow today could be the very thing that sets you back on track tomorrow.

STEP 4: IDENTIFYING WHAT CURRENTLY BRINGS YOU JOY

Joy isn't just about feeling good—it's also a key to understanding what brings you satisfaction and where your individual strengths and passions lie. When you take the time to identify what lights you up, you begin to uncover the activities, relationships and experiences that resonate most deeply with who you are. These moments of joy hold clues to your unique talents and the areas of life where you feel most aligned.

The joy you feel today is a compass pointing you toward your strengths. It's found in the things you love to do and the things you're naturally good at. Maybe you lose yourself in writing, gardening or problem-solving. Maybe it's in the satisfaction of helping others, organizing a space or learning something new. Whatever it is, these moments matter—they reveal the parts of your life where you thrive and where you find meaning.

REFLECTION EXERCISE: WHERE IS YOUR JOY?

Take a moment to reflect on what currently brings you joy. Grab your notebook or journal and write down your answers to the following questions:

1. What are three things you've done in the past week that made you feel happy, satisfied or accomplished?

2. When was the last time you felt completely engaged in something, as though time didn't matter? What were you doing?

3. Are there activities, hobbies, or moments in your daily life that feel effortless and fulfilling?

DISCOVERING PATTERNS AND STRENGTHS

After you've written down your answers, look for patterns. Are the things that bring you joy related to creativity, like painting or writing? Do they involve problem-solving, connecting with others or exploring new ideas? What about the feelings they inspire—do they make you feel energized, proud or at peace?

These patterns offer valuable insights into your individual strengths and passions. For example, if your joy often comes from helping others, it might point to a talent in teaching or solving problems or demonstrating compassion. If you feel satisfied after organizing a space, it could reveal a talent for creating order or designing systems.

CONNECTING JOY TO YOUR LIFE'S PATH

The purpose of identifying your current sources of joy isn't just to feel good (although I definitely want you to feel good)—it's to gain clarity about what aligns with your unique strengths and passions. When you recognize these things, you can begin to make intentional choices about where to focus your time and energy.

This week, pay attention to what brings you joy with an eye toward uncovering your personal strengths. Write these moments down, reflect on their patterns and consider how they might connect to your larger goals. By understanding what currently brings you joy, you'll take a powerful step toward aligning your life with your true self.

PRACTICAL FRAMEWORK:
YOUR SEASON AND JOY MAP

Now that you've explored your current season, identified what brings you joy and reflected on your strengths and passions, it's time to pull everything together into a practical framework. This map will help you understand where you are right now, what brings you fulfillment and how you can take actionable steps to create more alignment and joy in your life.

This framework isn't about perfection—it's about awareness and intention. By mapping your current season and joy, you'll gain clarity about what's working, what's holding you back and where to focus your energy moving forward.

YOUR SEASON AND JOY MAP WORKSHEET

Use the following columns to create your personalized map:

	EXAMPLE PROMPTS
Current Season	What season are you in (winter, spring, summer, fall)? Why do you feel this way?
Sources of Joy	What activities, relationships or experiences bring you joy or satisfaction?
Barriers to Joy	What's preventing you from experiencing joy? (e.g., time, mindset, responsibilities)
Small Actions to Priotize Joy	What small steps can you take to lean into your joy? (e.g., schedule time, say "yes" to opportunities, seek support)

EXAMPLE MAP

SEASON:	Winter	Spring	Fall
Sources of Joy	Reading, long walks, quiet reflection	Brainstorming ideas, learning new skills	Decluttering, organizing spaces
Barriers to Joy	Overworking, lack of energy	Fear of failure, procrastination	Feeling overwhelmed, lack of help
Small Actions to Priotize Joy	Set aside 15 minutes a day for a walk or reading break.	Dedicate one hour a week to explore a new project or hobby.	Tackle one small area per day (like a drawer or shelf).

HOW TO USE YOUR MAP

1. **Identify Your Current Season:** Reflect on your emotional, mental and physical state and decide which season you're in. Write it down in the first column.

2. **List Your Sources of Joy:** Pull from the exercises earlier in this chapter to list the activities, people or experiences that make you feel alive and fulfilled.

3. **Acknowledge Barriers to Joy:** Be honest about what's getting in the way. Is it lack of time, resources or energy? Is it fear, self-doubt or guilt? Naming your barriers is the first step to overcoming them.

4. **Plan Small Actions to Prioritize Joy:**
   Start small. What's one thing you can do today to create more space for joy in your life? Maybe it's scheduling 10 minutes to read, reconnecting with an old hobby or saying no to something that drains your energy.

WHAT DOES IT MEAN?
- Looking at your map, what stands out to you?
- Are there opportunities for joy that you've been overlooking?
- What small actions can you start taking this week to lean into your joy?

This map isn't set in stone—it's a living document. Your season will change and so will your sources of joy and barriers. Revisit this framework regularly to stay aligned with where you are and where you want to go. By using this map, you're taking meaningful steps toward living a life that feels deeply connected to your strengths, passions and purpose.

The first part of this process is to take a look back and do some self-reflection on what brought you to where you are now. Ready? Let's dive right in. ⚿

CHAPTER THREE

Early Glimmers

I WENT THROUGH school and even college without a single meaningful conversation about the things I enjoyed doing. Not one. The adults in my life never asked in any depth what I liked, what I was good at or what brought me joy. And honestly, I didn't ask myself either. Life wasn't about joy or interests; it was about practicality.

When I was five, saying I wanted to be an astronaut or doctor or TV newsperson was cute. People would smile and nod, but by the time I was older, it was a different story. Suddenly, the same adults who had once indulged my dreams were quick to dismiss them: "That'll never happen," "You're not good at some of those subjects," or the classic, "You can't make a living at that." In my house, the conversation revolved around what skills would get me a good, stable job—something better than farming, teaching or police work, which had been the family staples.

My mom did throw in one additional piece of advice: "Never depend on a man for money." Watching so many divorces—and eventually becoming part of that statistic her-self—left her with a realistic (if not entirely hopeful) outlook on finances. Self-reliance wasn't just a virtue in our house, it was a necessity. That practicality was drilled into me from the start.

But if I think back to being school-age, I still had things I loved. Riding my bike was freedom—a ticket to go wherever I wanted, as long as I raced home by sundown (the universal Gen X curfew). But I didn't want to be a professional cyclist. I liked eating cookies and sometimes I had the patience to make them. But becoming a baker? Nope.

Then there was my obsession with stickers. I had a full-blown girl crush on Lisa Frank—the OG technicolor queen of tween girl products in the '80s. I loved collecting her stickers and admiring her creations, but I couldn't figure out how to monetize my obsession. So, stickers stayed a hobby, not a ca-reer path.

And then there was my paternal grandmother, who once told me my talents in life were untying knots and having nice handwriting. Knots and handwriting. Really? Maybe there was a maritime or calligraphy career waiting for me, but it didn't exactly scream "big future." I always found that com-ment equal parts hilarious and baffling. Was this really the best assessment of my potential?

Despite all of this, a couple of things managed to stick. Two glimmers of talents survived the practicality filter: reading and looking stuff up. My mom was a high school English teacher, so books were everywhere. I devoured them.

Whether it was being an only child or just having a natural knack, I entertained myself by reading anything I could get my hands on.

Then there was my love of research, although I didn't recognize it as a "thing" back then. In the pre-internet days, being told to "go look it up" was basically a teacher or parental brush-off. But I took it seriously. I'd drag out the dusty encyclopedias and lose hours just flipping through pages because I found the information fascinating. I knew how to use the card catalog at the library and could hunt down books hidden in the stacks like a detective. I craved knowledge and had a talent for finding it.

Fast forward to today and my family laughs and says how I'm "good at Google." We all have the same Google, right? But somehow, I get results that no one else seems to find. Reading and researching—two glimmers that were there all along. I just didn't know what to do with them back then. They were little whispers, hints of something bigger, hiding in plain sight.

LET'S GET PRACTICAL

Somewhere along the way, most of us learn that dreaming big is a luxury, not an inherent right. When we're kids, the world feels wide open. We're encouraged to imagine ourselves as astronauts, artists, superheroes or anything we can dream up. But as we grow older, those same dreams start getting trimmed, reshaped and in some cases, outright dismissed.

It doesn't happen all at once. It's gradual, subtle. At first, your dreams are met with indulgent smiles and "Oh, how cute!" Then, the questions creep in: "But how will you earn a real living at that?" or "That's not realistic." By the time you hit your teens, the dismissal becomes more direct. In the story I just shared, I talked about how childhood dreams— like wanting to be an astronaut or doctor or TV newsperson—were met with phrases like "You're not good at some of those things" or "That'll never happen." These messages chisel away at our confidence until all that's left is the need to be "practical."

And it's not just family expectations. It's school, society, media—everywhere we turn, we're fed the idea that our worth is tied to practicality. Creative pursuits? A waste of time. Big dreams? Only for the lucky few. Anything that doesn't fit neatly into a career box? A cute hobby at best.

By the time we hit adulthood, we've so thoroughly absorbed these messages that we stop dreaming altogether. We don't raise our hands. We don't speak up. We tell ourselves it's because we've outgrown those silly, impractical ideas, but the truth is, we've been trained to believe they don't matter. And that belief doesn't just kill our dreams—it kills our spark, our joy and eventually, our sense of who we are.

But here's the thing: those dreams you had as a kid, those passions you buried under practicality, they didn't go away. They're still there, waiting for you to notice them again. The question is whether you're willing to dig them back up and give them the chance they deserved all along.

Because when you do, everything starts to change. And the best part? You don't have to pick between dreaming big and being practical—you can do both. It just starts with giving yourself permission to dream again.

WHAT DID YOU WANT TO BE?

Take a moment and think back to your childhood. Remember that time when anything seemed possible and you felt free to dream without limits. When you were five or six or nine years old, what did you want to be? Did you dream of being an astronaut? A musician? A superhero? Or maybe you had more creative answers—like a professional tree climber or the inventor of flying cars. Whatever it was, you believed in it with your whole heart.

Now, think about the things you loved to do back then. What made you lose track of time? Was it building forts in the backyard, drawing pictures, reading stories or playing sports? Maybe you loved organizing your toys or creating elaborate games with your friends. These moments, even the smallest ones, can hold clues about the talents and passions that shaped who you are.

As we grow up, it becomes so easy to forget those early dreams. Somewhere along the way, life gets practical and we learn to dismiss the things that once made us feel alive. But those dreams and talents you had as a child didn't disappear. They're still there, waiting for you to notice them again.

REFLECTION PROMPT

Let's pause and reconnect with that younger version of your-self—the one who believed anything was possible. Grab your notebook or journal and spend a few minutes reflecting on the following questions. Take your time answering these questions. Don't filter or edit yourself—this is your space to dream and remember.

1. **What were your childhood dreams?**
   Think about what you wanted to be when you grew up. What felt exciting or magical to you back then?

2. **What did you love doing?**
   What activities made you lose track of time? What did you do just for fun without worrying about being "good enough"?

3. What were you told you were good at?

Did a teacher, parent or friend ever point out a skill or talent you had? Even if it seemed small or random, write it down.

WHAT DID YOU DISCOVER?

Once you've finished, take a moment to look over what you've written. Can you spot any patterns or recurring themes? Are there dreams or activities that still light you up today? This is the first step in uncovering the parts of yourself that might have been buried under the noise of practicality and expectations.

Your childhood dreams matter, even if they feel distant or small. They're a window into your unique strengths and passions—and they're worth exploring again.

THE IMPACT OF FAMILIAL AND SOCIETAL EXPECTATIONS

Growing up, I was surrounded by strong women who set the bar sky-high. My mother, aunt and grandmother were trail-blazers in their own right, each with advanced degrees and professional careers at a time when women were still expected to prioritize family over ambition. My maternal grandmother, for instance, graduated college in 1933 and later earned her master's degree—a feat that was practically unheard of for women in her generation. These women taught me that education and career were non-negotiables. They didn't just talk about it; they modeled it, breaking barriers in their fields and contributing to their communities with tireless dedication.

Their strength came with expectations. The message I received was clear: to honor their sacrifices and their legacy, I needed to achieve even more. My success wasn't just about me; it was about proving that their perseverance had been worth it. They had paved the way for me to go further, achieve more and above all, never settle. While that kind of pressure can be inspiring, it can also feel suffocating. There wasn't room to falter, question or take the scenic route. There was only one path, forward.

These expectations became the foundation for nearly every decision I made. In eighth grade, I chose to leave my small-town school to attend a large high school in a neighboring city with a more rigorous academic program. No one told me I had to, but I knew it was the "right" thing to do. The same logic applied when I went to college. I didn't sign up for fun or exploratory classes like art or music appreciation—I packed my schedule with practical courses directly tied to my (initial) double degree in business and law. My choices weren't about passion or curiosity; they were about efficiency and getting ahead.

Even after graduating (with a degree in economics but minus law), this drive shaped my career path. I followed the same conveyor belt of ambition I'd been on since childhood, always chasing the next logical step. I worked hard, met expectations and excelled in environments where achievement was everything. But along the way, I never stopped to ask myself: *Is this what I really want?* The truth is, it never occurred to me that I could pause, recalibrate or even question whether I was on the right path. After all, this was what I'd been raised to do: keep going, keep achieving and don't look back.

GENERATIONAL VALUES: INSPIRATION AND CONSTRAINTS

The generational values I inherited—perseverance, self-reliance and a relentless work ethic—are deeply woven into the fabric of who I am. Watching my grandmother navigate a male-dominated world, my mother juggle work and divorce, and my aunt thrive in her legal career was both empowering and daunting. These women showed me that I could endure anything, achieve anything and that no obstacle was insurmountable. But there was a flip side to this resilience: it came with an unspoken rule that vulnerability and rest weren't options. Perseverance meant pushing through no matter what, even when it hurt.

While self-reliance was a gift that gave me confidence and independence, it also created walls. It kept me from asking for help or admitting when I needed it. I saw rest and reflection as luxuries I couldn't afford. Slowing down felt like failure. These values, as inspiring as they were, often made me feel like I had to carry the weight of the world alone. It took years—and a lot of soul-searching—to realize that the very traits that propelled me forward could also hold me back. To grow, I had to embrace the idea that resilience wasn't just about endurance; it was also about knowing when to stop, breathe and choose a new path.

THE CONSULTING JOB: BILLABLE HOURS OVER WELL-BEING

I'll never forget a conversation I had early in my consulting career, my first job out of college. My team leader informed me, without a hint of irony, that I needed to handle everything outside of my billable hours—email, training, even being sick—on my "own time." Apparently, the expectation was to dedicate a minimum of 50 hours a week to clients and anything else, including basic self-care, was an afterthought. The unspoken message was clear: if you couldn't keep up, it was a personal failing, not a flaw in the system.

What's more, the company celebrated people who worked 100-hour weeks, handing out awards as if overwork was a badge of honor. At the time, I didn't question it. Like so many others, I internalized the pressure and pushed myself to meet impossible standards. But looking back, I can see how damaging that culture was—not just to my physical and mental health but to my sense of worth. It didn't matter that I was successful on paper. The constant grind left no room for reflection, connection or joy. I was burned out, isolated and, worst of all, completely numb to the things that used to make me feel alive.

THE CONSEQUENCES OF IGNORING JOY

Ignoring joy and personal interests in favor of external validation is like building a house without a foundation. It might stand for a while, but eventually, the cracks will start to show. For me, those cracks appeared as exhaustion, disengagement and a gnawing sense that something was missing. I was so focused on meeting expectations and earning approval that I didn't realize how much I was sacrificing in the process. The longer I ignored my own needs and passions, the more disconnected I felt—from myself, my work and even the people around me.

This constant pursuit of achievement without joy doesn't just take a toll on your mental health; it erodes your sense of identity. You stop asking questions like *What do I love?* or *What makes me feel alive?* because there's no time to consider them. Instead, you wake up one day and realize you don't recognize the person in the mirror. For me, it took a long time to see that success at the expense of my well-being wasn't really success at all.

RETURNING TO THE GROCERY STORE

I can't think about the disconnect between personal interests and job demands without going back to that moment in the grocery store—the one that stopped me in my tracks. Standing there in the frozen foods aisle, face to face with a man whose life I'd upended just weeks earlier, was a brutal wake-up call. His name was Brian and I didn't even remember him. That realization hit me like a freight train: I had fired so many people that it didn't even register as unique anymore. I was numb, moving through life on autopilot, completely detached from the weight of what I was doing.

That encounter forced me to reckon with the truth I had been avoiding for years. My work, the very thing I'd built my life around, didn't align with who I was or what I cared about. I had become a cog in a system that prioritized efficiency over humanity and I was complicit in it. The job was practical, prestigious and paid well—everything I'd been taught to value. But it drained me. It left no room for joy, connection or purpose. The grocery store moment wasn't just about Brian; it was about me finally seeing the cost of living a life out of alignment with my true self.

Looking back, that moment was the beginning of a shift. It planted a seed of awareness—a flicker of understanding that things didn't have to stay the same. I didn't quit my job the next day or march into my boss's office demanding change. But I did start to notice the cracks in the facade I'd built around my life. That single encounter opened my eyes to the toll of ignoring my joy and passions and, while I didn't know it then, it set me on a path toward something better. This chapter is about that journey—how I began to peel back the layers of what wasn't working and take small, deliberate steps toward a life that did.

CHANGE STARTS SMALL

When we think about monumental change, we often picture dramatic, Hollywood-style moments—a grand gesture, a bold decision or an overnight transformation that instantly turns everything around. But in real life, change rarely works that way. It's not a single moment that redefines everything but a series of small shifts, tiny realizations and deliberate choices that build on each other over time. It's less about flipping a switch and more about planting seeds—seeds that might take weeks, months or even years to grow into something meaningful.

That's why it's so important to pay attention to the moments that invite awareness. They might feel small or fleeting, like an encounter that makes you uncomfortable or a lingering sense that something isn't working. But those moments are opportunities—signposts pointing toward the possibility of change. It's easy to dismiss them, to get caught up in the day-to-day grind and ignore the whispers that tell you something could be different. Yet, it's those whispers that plant the seeds of transformation. And when you water them with intention, they can grow into something extraordinary.

THE POWER OF INTENTIONAL LIVING

Living intentionally is the key to cultivating those seeds. It means making deliberate choices that align with your values, passions and authentic self. It's about stepping off autopilot, examining the life you're living and taking ownership of your decisions—no matter how small. You don't need a perfectly mapped-out plan or the answers to every question. Living intentionally is more about awareness and courage than certainty. It's about noticing the areas of your life that feel out of sync and making choices that honor who you are and what you truly want.

These small, intentional actions might seem minor in the moment—carving out 15 minutes to reconnect with a hobby, saying no to an unnecessary obligation or pausing to reflect on what feels fulfilling. But over time, they create a ripple effect, shifting the trajectory of your life.

By living with intention, you give yourself the power to align your life with your values and purpose, creating room for joy, growth and transformation. And as those small steps accumulate, they lead to profound, lasting change—proof that the journey is just as important as the destination.

HOW DO YOU BEGIN?

My journey toward alignment didn't start with a grand epiphany or an immediate life overhaul—it began with something much smaller: paying attention to the quiet inner voice that had been there all along. For years, I had ignored it, burying it beneath the noise of external expectations and the demands of daily life. But after that grocery store moment, I couldn't silence it anymore. It whispered questions like *What if things could be different?* and *What if there's another way?*

At first, I didn't have answers, but I realized the act of listening was a step in itself. That small shift in awareness opened a door I hadn't known was there.

Around this time, I came across a book that would change the way I saw myself: *Now, Discover Your Strengths* by Dr. Don Clifton and Marcus Buckingham. The book introduced me to the StrengthsFinder® assessment, a tool designed to identify and articulate individual strengths.

I was skeptical at first—how could a simple assessment possibly capture what made me unique? But as I read the book and took the assessment, I was blown away by its accuracy. It didn't just confirm things I already knew about myself; it gave me a language to describe them and a framework to understand them. For the first time, I had words to explain my natural tendencies, the things I excelled at and the ways I could lean into those strengths in my personal and professional life.

That experience was more than just eye-opening—it was validating. For so long, I had been chasing external markers of success, trying to fit into roles that didn't align with who I truly was. Discovering my strengths felt like coming home to myself. It was a moment of clarity that helped me see that I wasn't broken or unfit for the roles I'd taken on—I simply hadn't been working in a way that honored my natural talents.

That realization was a game-changer. It didn't solve everything overnight, but it gave me a foundation to start building a life that felt more authentic, intentional and aligned with who I was at my core. And that made all the difference.

Discovering and understanding your strengths isn't just a feel-good exercise—it's a proven way to improve your quality of life and career satisfaction. According to Gallup, people who understand their strengths are three times as likely to report a higher quality of life and six times as likely to feel engaged in their jobs. When you know what you're naturally good at and how to apply it, you're more likely to find fulfillment and purpose in your work and personal life.

REFLECTION ACTIVITY:
VISUALIZING THE BENEFITS OF ALIGNMENT

This simple activity will help you explore how bringing your life into alignment with your talents and joys could positively impact different areas of your life.

STEP 1: IMAGINE YOUR ALIGNED LIFE

Take a few moments to close your eyes and visualize what your life might look like if it were in full alignment with your talents and the things that bring you joy. Picture yourself:

- Doing work that energizes you and feels meaningful.
- Spending time on hobbies or activities that light you up.
- Feeling a sense of purpose and fulfillment in your daily life.

What do you see? How does it feel to live that way?

STEP 2: REFLECT ON KEY AREAS

In your journal or notebook, write down your thoughts about how alignment could improve these areas of your life:

- **Work:** How would your career or daily responsibilities feel different if they aligned with your strengths and passions?
- **Relationships:** How might your connections with others change if you were more joyful and fulfilled?
- **Personal Well-Being:** How would alignment affect your mental, emotional and physical health?

STEP 3: WRITE A "FUTURE SNAPSHOT"

Now, write a few sentences describing your ideal day in a life aligned with your talents and joys. Be as specific as you can. For example:

- "I wake up feeling excited about the work ahead, knowing it aligns with my strengths. I spend time doing things I love, like painting and spending time with friends, and end the day feeling accomplished and at peace."

STEP 4: IDENTIFY KEY BENEFITS

After completing your snapshot, reflect on the specific ways this aligned life would benefit you. Write down your thoughts:

- What would you gain emotionally?
- How would your relationships improve?
- How would your sense of purpose and fulfillment grow?

This activity isn't just about dreaming—it's about creating a vision for what alignment could look like and giving yourself the motivation to pursue it. The clearer you are about the benefits, the easier it will be to take the first steps toward making that vision a reality. In the next chapter, we'll do some fun exercises to help you identify your strengths and how you might lean into them to bring your life into better alignment with your authentic self. 🔑

CHAPTER FOUR

The Keys

ONE OF THE most common sentiments I hear from coaching clients is this: *"I feel like I'm not where I'm supposed to be."* Maybe you've felt this way too—a nagging sense that your current situation doesn't quite fit, that something is missing or that life feels like it's happening *to* you rather than *for* you. When I ask these clients where they want to be, the answer is often a hesitant, "I'm not sure. Just … not here."

If that resonates with you, take a deep breath. You're not alone and it's okay not to have all the answers right now. You don't need to have your entire future mapped out today. What matters is that you're here, willing to explore and take the first steps toward something better. This chapter will introduce tools you can use to create a roadmap to move toward an aligned life with intention and clarity.

Here's the thing about alignment: it's not a destination. It's not a mythical point in the future where everything mag- ically falls into place and you finally feel fulfilled. Alignment is a state of being on the journey—something you build into your life each day through small, intentional choices. Life is happening right now, in this moment. Waiting for the stars to align isn't a strategy; it's a hope. And while hope can inspire us, it's not enough on its own. A plan is actionable. A plan gives you a sense of control over your life's direction, helping you create the change you crave.

In this chapter, we'll begin that process. Together, we'll start to uncover where you want to go and how you can get there. We'll explore practical strategies to help you navigate this journey, one step at a time. Because alignment isn't about waiting for life to happen—it's about actively shaping it in a way that reflects your values, talents and joys.

REMEMBERING YOUR JOY

We're going to learn about a set of alignment strategies I call the "keys" that will help you begin the process of uncovering your authentic self so you can align your life with who you are at your core. But first, let's revisit a concept we discussed in a previous chapter—the unfiltered confidence and joy we experienced as children. This idea isn't just a nostalgic reflection; it's a foundational piece of the alignment process, offering a lens through which we can reconnect with the parts of ourselves that may have been overshadowed by societal expectations and self-doubt.

Think back to childhood, when you embraced your talents and joys without hesitation or self-judgment. As kids, we had an innate sense of confidence in our abilities, whether it was declaring ourselves the best at making macaroni and cheese, crafting elaborate stories or racing bikes down the street. There was no filter, no internal voice whispering, *"That's not good enough,"* or *"You shouldn't like that."* We simply followed what brought us joy.

Now, as adults, that confidence can feel like a distant memory. Instead of proudly naming our talents, we hesitate, second-guess ourselves and often dismiss the things we're naturally good at as "insignificant" or "impractical." This shift isn't accidental—it's the result of years of societal conditioning, where external voices told us to prioritize practicality over passion, conformity over individuality.

It's no wonder our levels of engagement start high and drop off precipitously over time! Remember the Gallup study we saw in Chapter Two that showed that by the time we're heading toward college, trade school or our careers, we've long since stopped dreaming about the things that excited us or brought us joy as children. It showed that we've stopped confidently claiming the things we're good at, unless those things contribute to something society deems productive and practical.

Wouldn't it be wonderful to feel that confident and connected to our inner selves again? Recalling your glimmers of joy and your childhood confidence is the first step toward reclaiming the parts of ourselves that have been quieted over time.

This is where the keys come in. They are a framework designed to help you reconnect with those sparks of joy and confidence, then build on them intentionally. These strategies will guide you in uncovering who you truly are, aligning your life with your authentic self and creating a path forward that feels both purposeful and fulfilling. By revisiting what once came naturally to you and applying the tools in this framework, you'll be able to navigate the journey of alignment with clarity and intention.

I want to be clear about something: alignment isn't a finish line. It's a daily practice. A choice you make again and again. It's not about perfection; it's about intention. And it's absolutely possible, no matter where you're starting from.

Let's take a closer look at how the keys work, their purpose and how they can help you begin to live a life that reflects your true self.

INTRODUCING THE FRAMEWORK

Over the years, through personal trial and error and countless conversations with coaching clients, I've developed a framework that has helped me—and so many others—move toward alignment. I call these strategies "the keys" because they are exactly that: tools to unlock the potential within you and open the doors to a life that feels aligned with your values, talents and joys. These keys aren't a one-size-fits-all solution; they're adaptable, practical and designed to meet you wherever you are on your journey.

KEY 1: THE WHISPERS.

There's a quiet voice that calls out to each of us—the gentle tug in our hearts that draws us toward the activities and ideas that light us up. It's not always a shout; in fact, it's usually just a whisper. But if we slow down and pay attention, that persistent longing can guide us to our most authentic and powerful talents. Some people call them "yearnings," but I like to say it's about listening for the whispers. Whether it's that urge to write, the pull to create or the spark of energy you feel when helping others, these subtle signals are often the first clue that you're on the path to a life fully aligned with who you really are. Don't dismiss them as daydreams—honor them. They may well be the keys that unlock your greatest potential.

KEY 2: YOUR LIKES.

These are often overlooked but there is tremendous power in simply knowing what you like. While it sounds obvious, many people struggle to name what genuinely brings them joy after years of prioritizing performance, responsibility and external validation. That's why we've spent so much time talking about it—it is that fundamental to the work. Understanding your likes is a critical step in reclaiming alignment, as these preferences serve as breadcrumbs back to your authentic self.

KEY 3: INDICATORS.

These are emotional signals that help you recognize whether you are aligned—or misaligned—with your values, goals and personal strengths. They're the early-warning system of your internal world, alerting you to what's going on beneath the surface. These feelings can be positive, negative or even neutral, but what makes them "indicators" is the way they guide your awareness and prompt you to take action or make a shift.

KEY 4: EMOTIONS.

Emotions—especially the uncomfortable ones—are not problems to fix but signals to interpret. Learn to recognize your own "indicator feelings"—like dread, fatigue, resentment or numbness—as internal messages pointing to areas of misalignment. The cognitive behavioral triangle (thoughts, feelings, behaviors) can help us catch ourselves earlier, avoid spirals and begin realigning before burnout sets in. Emotions become less like red flags and more like road signs—guides that help us course-correct toward what matters most.

KEY 5: SCOUTS.

All too often, we're so busy pushing forward that we forget to notice who's cheering us on or where that applause is coming from. I'm talking about the people around you who see something special in you before you even realize it's there—your scouts. They're the ones who recognize your natural abilities, offer encouragement and maybe even nudge you toward opportunities you hadn't considered. They might see the budding passion or hidden talent that you can't yet put your finger on, providing valuable clues that direct you toward a life that's in true harmony with your strengths.

KEY 6: ENGAGEMENT.

Engagement is more than a corporate buzzword—it's a deeply personal metric for alignment. Whether it's parenting, friend-ships or creative pursuits, you will learn to assess your own energy states across green (energized), yellow (checked out) and red (drained) zones. Let's begin to understand where our energy is leaking—and how to reclaim it. Energy is data and noticing your state of being is a critical step toward living a more aligned, intentional life.

KEY 7: YOUR BEST DAY.

Here we will explore in detail what made that day great— was it the people, the pace, the creativity, the quiet? These moments aren't accidental; they're clues. By examining these peak experiences, you can learn to replicate the ingredients in your current life, creating intentional momentum toward sus-tained alignment. This chapter is both practical and empow-ering: your best day isn't a fluke—it's a blueprint.

KEY 8: FUTURE CASTING.

We get to design our roadmap—that's amazing news! We get to set the destination and then plan the route. So we need to be clear on where we are going, adjust on the way to deal with things as they come up and look to role models to help. Ask yourself along the way, "is this taking me closer to or further away" from my goal? And not just a point on a map but also how will my life look, feel or be different? How can I keep that vision front and center?

KEY 9: YOUR BODY RESPONSES.

Your body is talking to you, are you listening? Often-ignored signals of the body—tight shoulders, racing thoughts, gut reactions—are valuable sources of data. Let's tune into our internal cues with cognitive behavioral principles and ultra-dian rhythm research. By understanding how our bodies react to stress, excitement or depletion, we gain an early-warning system for misalignment and a more compassionate way to check in with ourselves before burnout hits.

KEY 10: ULTRADIAN RHYTHMS.

Here's a biological truth: humans are designed to move in waves. Enter ultradian rhythms—natural 90- to 120-minute cycles of energy, clarity and fatigue. Let's honor our body's signals and plan our day around peak focus periods and develop a more sustainable, humane way to work. Rest becomes strategic. Energy becomes the new time. And honoring your rhythm becomes an act of courage not indulgence.

KEY 11: YOUR GIFTS.
Your natural talents aren't random—they're your biggest clues to alignment. And burnout often results from working out of our "zones of competence" rather than "zones of genius." Let's reclaim our gifts that we may have taken for granted and start building a life around what energizes rather than depletes.

KEY 12: BOUNDARIES.
Boundaries are absolutely transformative. They are intentional lines that protect your energy, values and well-being. They're not selfish—they're essential. Let's recognize where you might be overextending yourself and learn how to start saying yes only to what aligns. Every time you set a boundary, you reinforce the message: "I matter here."

Think of these keys as a compass, guiding you step by step through the process of aligning your life with your authentic self. Each one builds upon the others, offering insights and strategies to help you clarify your goals, navigate challenges and create a life that feels more fulfilling. This framework isn't about perfection or a linear path—it's about equipping you with the tools to make intentional choices, even in the face of uncertainty.

THE PURPOSE OF THE KEYS

At their core, the keys serve three main purposes:

1. **Identifying Your Alignment Journey**

   The first step to creating a life that feels aligned is understanding what alignment looks like for you. This framework helps you dig deep into your inner voice, uncovering the whispers and sparks of joy that often go unnoticed in the noise of daily life. Through reflection and practical exercises, you'll begin to paint a clearer picture of where you want to go—and why it matters.

2. **Working Through Challenges**

   Let's be honest: alignment isn't always easy. Life throws curveballs, self-doubt creeps in and societal pressures can make you second-guess yourself. These keys are designed to help you navigate those obstacles with resilience and clarity. They offer a roadmap to keep you focused, even when the journey feels overwhelming.

3. **Creating a New Normal**

   Alignment isn't a one-time event; it's a way of life. The keys will help you establish new habits, mindsets and practices that support your ongoing journey. By integrating these strategies into your daily routine, you'll create a sustainable foundation for growth and fulfillment, allowing you to thrive in alignment with your authentic self.

UNLOCKING YOUR INNER VOICE WITH PURPOSE AND INTENTION

The heart of this framework is the belief that your inner voice matters. That small, persistent whisper—the one that tells you there's more to life than what you're experiencing right now— is worth listening to. The keys will help you give life to that voice, amplifying it so that it becomes a guiding force in your decisions and actions.

But listening to your inner voice is only the beginning. Alignment requires purposeful action. These keys aren't just about dreaming; they're about doing. They're about creating a plan and taking tangible steps toward the life you envision. Each key is a reminder that you are in control of your journey and that by living intentionally, you can align your life with what truly matters to you.

As we explore each key in the coming chapters, remember that this process is uniquely yours. There's no right or wrong way to use these tools—only the way that works best for you. My goal is to empower you with strategies that inspire confidence, clarity and momentum, so you can move forward with purpose and intention. Let's start unlocking the doors to your aligned life together. 🔑

CHAPTER FIVE

Key: The Whispers

IN OUR JOURNEY toward alignment, one of the most powerful tools we can learn to recognize is the concept of whispers. Whispers are those subtle, intuitive nudges or messages that seem to call out to us—quiet invitations to explore new possibilities or gentle warnings to tread carefully. They aren't loud, dramatic declarations or grand gestures; instead, they're fleeting thoughts, moments of curiosity or a persistent pull toward something we can't quite define.

These whispers are often glimpses of something yet to be discovered. They might show up as a feeling of excitement when you think about trying something new, an unexpected connection you can't shake or even a quiet voice in your head suggesting, "Maybe this is worth exploring."

On the flip side, whispers can also act as warning signs—moments of discomfort or unease that signal misalignment. Either way, whispers are incredibly valuable because they act as guideposts, gently nudging us closer to our authentic selves.

It's important to differentiate whispers from what I like to call "Hollywood moments." In movies, life-changing decisions often follow dramatic events—a booming voice in the sky, a sudden epiphany or a clear and unmistakable sign of what to do next. Think of the movie "Field of Dreams," where Kevin Costner's character hears a mysterious voice in the corn field telling him "If you build it, they will come." Whispers are nothing like that. They aren't flashy or overwhelming; they're subtle and often easy to overlook. You won't find a spotlight shining on the answer or a voiceover explaining your next step. Instead, whispers require us to slow down, pay attention and trust our intuition. They are quiet but persistent, waiting for us to notice and respond.

The magic of whispers lies in their ability to connect us with our deeper truths. They bypass the noise of daily life and cut through the expectations of others, offering us a moment of clarity about what resonates with who we are at our core. By tuning into these whispers, we can begin to uncover the possibilities and paths that align with our values, talents and passions—paths we might never have considered otherwise.

EARLY WHISPERS OF ENTREPRENEURSHIP

Looking back, I can see that whispers of entrepreneurship had been calling to me long before I even recognized them as such. These subtle nudges showed up in small but intriguing ways, like hobbies that seemed to spark curiosity and excitement. One of the earliest examples was a quirky little project I started in the early 2000s—a "best of" rudimentary website where I mused about my favorite discoveries, on everything from steakhouses to notebooks to paper towels. It was purely for fun, but I can see now that it reflected something deeper: my love for identifying quality, sharing insights and curating experiences.

At the time, I had no idea this project could lead anywhere. Influencer culture wasn't a thing yet and social media platforms like Facebook and Instagram were not yet around. Still, the process of creating and sharing my opinions as a way to help others gave me a sense of joy and purpose. Even though I didn't realize it then, this was a whisper—a glimpse of a potential path where I could combine my passion for organization and creativity with my knack for connecting people to ideas.

Later, another whisper surfaced when I explored the world of professional organizing. I loved organizing my own space and often found myself drawn to the aisles of The Container Store or HGTV shows about decluttering and design. This interest grew into action when I attended a week-long certification program for professional organizers and even launched a small business called "Solutions 4 Living." I had the logo, the business cards and a binder full of systems and methodologies. My first big client was a local radio personality, and I dove into the project with high hopes.

But as much as I loved the *idea* of organizing, I quickly realized I didn't love the actual *work* of organizing for others. Sorting through other people's clutter, navigating their emotional attachment to "stuff," and the physical demands of the job weren't a fit for me. It was a tough realization and I initially felt like I had failed. But over time, I came to understand that this experience was invaluable. It wasn't a failure; it was another whisper—one that clarified what I didn't want and helped me refine what I was truly drawn to: creating systems, solving problems and designing solutions, but on my own terms. I wanted to be an example and inspiration for others to use as they embarked on their own journeys, rather than do the work for them.

These early whispers weren't fully formed or definitive, but they planted seeds of possibility. They nudged me to explore, experiment and take risks, even if the outcomes weren't always what I expected. Each step brought me closer to understanding what alignment might look like for me and how I could build a life that reflected my values, talents and joys.

POSITIVE WHISPERS: INVITATIONS TO EXPLORE

Positive whispers often present themselves as sparks of curiosity or interest. They might not point to a fully formed goal, but they draw us toward something that resonates with our values or natural abilities. For me, one of those whispers emerged as a love for creating systems and solutions. Whether it was through experimenting with a "best of" website or diving into professional organizing, I felt a pull toward identifying patterns, solving problems and making life more streamlined.

At the time, I didn't have a clear vision of how these interests could evolve into something meaningful. I only knew that these activities brought me joy and a sense of purpose. Over time, however, these whispers crystallized into a passion for leadership development. I realized that what I loved wasn't necessarily the act of organizing or curating lists—it was the deeper work of helping others design processes, clear roadblocks and unlock their potential. Those early whispers were breadcrumbs, guiding me toward a career that would align with my values and strengths.

CAUTIONARY WHISPERS: WARNINGS TO HEED

Not all whispers point us toward something new; some warn us away from choices that might lead to frustration or mis-alignment. These cautionary whispers are just as important as the positive ones, helping us refine our path and avoid detours that don't serve us. My exploration of professional organizing was a perfect example of this. At first, the idea felt exciting and aligned with my love for order and design. But when I dove into the work, I quickly realized it wasn't quite the right fit.

What seemed like a dream on paper turned out to be a mismatch in practice. I didn't enjoy the physical demands (cleaning out and schlepping heavy boxes, working in hot at-tics and garages), the emotional labor of helping others part with their belongings or the limitations of being tied to hourly work. That whisper wasn't telling me to stop exploring—it was telling me to redirect my energy. It taught me to focus on the elements I did enjoy, like devising solutions and streamlining processes, while leaving behind the parts that didn't align with my strengths or long-term goals.

LISTENING TO BOTH TYPES OF WHISPERS

Whether they're urging you forward or cautioning you to pause, whispers are invaluable tools for self-discovery. Positive whispers help you uncover what resonates, even if you don't yet know how to act on it. Cautionary whispers, on the other hand, save you from investing time and energy into paths that aren't meant for you. Both types are essential for navigating your alignment journey with clarity and intention. By listening to these quiet messages and reflecting on what they're telling you, you can move closer to a life that truly reflects your authentic self.

KYLA'S STORY

Kyla's talent for coaching and supporting others was evident long before she recognized it as a viable career path. Throughout her corporate roles in communications and speechwriting, she became the go-to person for colleagues navigating career transitions. Whether it was helping someone reframe their résumé, strategize for a promotion or plan a career pivot, Kyla had an intuitive ability to guide others toward clarity and confidence.

She wasn't advertising herself as a coach; in fact, at the time, she didn't even consider coaching as a profession.

But the whispers were there. Her natural aptitude for understanding people's potential and helping them position themselves for success surfaced repeatedly, even when her job descriptions had nothing to do with this skill set.

As Kyla advanced in her corporate career and became a people manager, these whispers grew louder. In one-on-one meetings with her direct reports, conversations often shifted from performance feedback to larger coaching discussions about career aspirations and personal fulfillment. She found herself not only supporting her team members in their current roles but also guiding them toward opportunities beyond the company, sometimes coaching them to leave entirely. Although she wasn't yet labeling herself a coach, her actions spoke volumes about where her true strengths and passions lay.

THE TURNING POINT

Eventually, Kyla began to notice a stark contrast between her corporate job and the work that brought her joy. The demands of her role were draining, leaving her unfulfilled and increasingly disconnected from her purpose. Yet, every time she helped someone gain clarity and take a meaningful step in their career, she felt alive. Coaching wasn't just something she was good at—it was something she couldn't stop doing. It gave her energy and a sense of deep satisfaction that her day job couldn't match.

Kyla's turning point came when she realized the misalignment between her corporate career and her natural talents. She recognized that coaching wasn't just a hobby or an occasional side activity—it was the work she was meant to do. Encouraged by the whispers and the feedback she'd received from colleagues and friends over the years, she made the bold decision to leave her corporate role and fully embrace coaching as her career. It wasn't an easy leap, but it was one she knew she needed to make to align her life with her passions.

THE OUTCOME

Today, Kyla runs a thriving coaching business that allows her to live in alignment with her values and talents. She specializes in helping women in corporate roles uncover their purpose and build careers that bring them joy and fulfillment--careers that often turn out to be entrepreneurial adventures. Best of all, Kyla designed her business to reflect her love for travel and flexibility. She and her husband now split their time between their lakeside home in Texas and a cabin in the Colorado mountains, with frequent trips to other destinations. Her coaching programs, including one aptly named *Your Radiant Mind*, are a testament to the clarity and alignment she's achieved by following her whispers.

Kyla's story is a powerful reminder of the importance of listening to those subtle nudges that point us toward our authentic selves. By embracing the clues her whispers offered, Kyla was able to leave a draining environment and create a life that reflects her values, passions and unique gifts. Her journey shows that when we trust the whispers and take intentional steps toward alignment, we can build a life that feels both purposeful and fulfilling.

THE ROLE OF REFLECTION AND RESILIENCE

REFRAMING MISSTEPS

Following whispers isn't always a straight path to success, but it is never wasted.

Sometimes, the pursuit of a whisper leads to an unexpected outcome or reveals that what initially seemed promising isn't the right fit. These moments, often labeled as "missteps" or "failures," are actually rich opportunities for growth and refinement.

Take my experience with professional organizing. Initially, the whisper to explore this path was exciting—it aligned with my love for order and creating systems. I even took concrete steps to build my skills, attending certification programs, designing a logo and completing projects. However, once I began the actual work of organizing for clients, I discovered it wasn't the right fit. The emotional toll of decluttering others' belongings and dealing with differing opinions made the work feel burdensome rather than fulfilling.

At first, this realization felt like a failure. But upon reflection, it became clear that the whisper wasn't wrong—it just pointed me toward something broader. The process helped clarify what I didn't want while highlighting elements I did value, such as creating solutions and developing systems. These insights became stepping stones toward building my leadership development business, which aligns deeply with my strengths and passions. This reframing of "missteps" as valuable data is a crucial part of the journey toward alignment.

GATHERING INSIGHTS

The key to learning from whispers—whether they lead to success or setbacks—is reflection. By taking the time to examine your experiences, you can identify patterns, refine your direction and better understand what truly resonates with you. Reflection isn't about dwelling on what went wrong; it's about extracting the lessons that can guide you forward.

Consider the role of resilience in this process. Staying open to the possibility that not every whisper will lead to immediate alignment requires courage and a willingness to adapt. Each experience, whether positive or challenging, offers insights into your values, talents and preferences. For instance, my experience with professional organizing didn't lead to a career in that field, but it provided valuable clarity on what I truly wanted in my work: autonomy, creativity and the ability to solve meaningful problems. Those principles come up over and over in my work with clients.

Resilience also means staying curious and willing to explore new whispers, even after encountering setbacks. The process of alignment is iterative—it involves testing, reflecting and adjusting as you gather more information about yourself and your desires. By approaching each step with an open mind and a commitment to learning, you can use your experiences to refine your journey and stay aligned with your authentic self.

Ultimately, whispers are not about perfection or a guaranteed outcome. They are about exploration, discovery and growth. When paired with reflection and resilience, they become powerful tools for navigating your journey toward alignment, helping you uncover the life that feels most authentic and fulfilling.

TUNING INTO YOUR WHISPERS

As we bring this chapter to a close, I want to encourage you to pause and listen. Whispers are subtle, often fleeting and easy to dismiss in the noise of daily life. But tuning into these intuitive nudges is a skill you can cultivate—a way of reconnecting with your inner compass. These whispers aren't random; they are messages from your authentic self, gently guiding you toward possibilities that align with who you are at your core.

Trusting your whispers requires courage. It's not about having all the answers or knowing exactly where they will lead. It's about being curious and open to what they reveal, even if it feels unfamiliar or uncertain. Every whisper is an opportunity to take a step closer to a life that reflects your true values and purpose.

Remember, alignment is not a one-time decision or a destination. It's an ongoing journey, made up of small, intentional steps. Each whisper you tune into and explore is part of that journey—part of building a life that feels deeply fulfilling and true to you.

EXERCISE: WHISPER MAPPING

This exercise will help you identify the whispers in your life and explore the possibilities they might hold. Set aside 15–20 minutes for this activity and find a quiet space where you can reflect without distractions.

STEP 1: CAPTURE THE WHISPERS

Divide a piece of paper or a journal page into two columns:

- **Positive Whispers:** On the left side, list any ideas, interests or opportunities that intrigue or excite you. These could be as simple as wanting to learn a new skill or as big as starting a business.

- **Cautionary Whispers:** On the right side, write down any nagging feelings of discomfort, unease or dissatisfaction. These might point to situations or paths that don't align with your values or joy.

STEP 2: EXPLORE THE PATTERNS

Once you've written down your whispers, reflect on what stands out. Ask yourself:

- Are there recurring themes or areas of interest?
- Do any of the whispers feel especially urgent or exciting?

- Are there whispers that signal it might be time to re-evaluate a certain aspect of your life?

STEP 3: TAKE A SMALL STEP

Choose one whisper from your list—positive or cautionary—and brainstorm a small, actionable step you can take to explore it further. For example:

- If a positive whisper is nudging you to try painting, commit to signing up for a beginner class.
- If a cautionary whisper is warning you about a draining relationship, think about setting a boundary or having an honest conversation.

STEP 4: REFLECT AND REPEAT

At the end of the week, revisit your list. Reflect on how tuning into that whisper impacted your perspective or choices. Did it provide clarity? Open a new door? Strengthen your intuition?

Make a habit of checking in with your whispers regularly. Over time, you'll notice how they begin to shape your journey, guiding you toward greater alignment with your authentic self.

By trusting your whispers and remaining open to their possibilities, you are giving yourself the gift of living intentionally. Each whisper is a step closer to the life you're meant to lead—a life that aligns with your true values, passions, and purpose. Listen closely. Your next step is waiting. ⚷

CHAPTER SIX

Key: Your Likes

AS WE CONTINUE this journey toward alignment, let's take a moment to reflect on where we've been. In the last chapter, we explored the concept of whispers—those subtle nudges that pull us toward something new or warn us when we're veering off course. Whispers help us notice possibilities, but awareness alone isn't enough. We need to take those insights further, turning them into tangible clues about what truly aligns with who we are.

One of the most fundamental yet overlooked keys to alignment is understanding what we actually *like*. This sounds simple enough—until you try to answer the question for yourself. What do you genuinely enjoy? What activities light you up? What brings you a sense of satisfaction, curiosity or fulfillment?

For many of us, this is where we hit a wall. Years of prioritizing external expectations—pleasing others, performing well checking the right boxes—have conditioned us to downplay or completely ignore our own preferences. Instead of focusing on what we like, we've learned to focus on what's practical, what's expected or what will bring approval.

When I ask clients the simple question, "What do you like?" I'm often met with hesitation, followed by an exasperated, "I don't know." Others answer with a dismissive, "Nothing," as if the ability to enjoy something has been buried under the weight of responsibility, productivity and obligation. And I get it—when we've spent so much time making choices based on what we *should* do, it can be incredibly difficult to shift our focus to what we *want* to do.

But here's the truth: Identifying what we like is not a frivolous exercise. It's essential. Our likes are more breadcrumbs leading us back to ourselves, revealing what brings us energy, excitement and meaning. If we ignore them, we risk building lives that feel successful on paper but empty in reality.

This is where a key distinction comes in: *what we like* is not always the same as *what we're good at*. It's entirely possible to be highly skilled at something and not enjoy it at all. In fact, many of us find ourselves trapped in jobs, roles, or responsibilities simply because we excel at them—not because they bring us fulfillment. And the more we perform well in these areas, the more we get asked (or expected) to do them. Without realizing it, we build a life around competence instead of passion.

That's why it's so important to consciously choose tasks and pursuits that align with genuine enjoyment. It's not enough to ask, *Am I good at this*? We also have to ask, *Do I actually like doing this*? Because if we don't make that distinction, we risk spending our days excelling at things that drain us, rather than thriving in things that excite us.

In this chapter, we're going to break that cycle. We'll separate what we *like* from what we're merely *good at*, helping us uncover the activities, interests and experiences that bring genuine joy. This isn't about what's "useful" or "profitable" in the eyes of the world—this is about you. Let's get started.

THE DIFFERENCE BETWEEN COMPETENCE AND PASSION

For a good part of my corporate career, I held the role of HR business partner, which meant I was embedded in a client group rather than identifying with corporate HR. I loved the role—most of the time. But there was one particular task I dreaded every year: pay planning.

Each year, we were handed a budget and expected to allocate raises and bonuses for every employee, balancing performance ratings, market value, individual aspirations and business priorities in a complex, high-stakes puzzle. It was a soul-sucking, zero-sum game, where giving someone a higher increase meant taking from someone else. The process was also manual, requiring endless spreadsheets with macros and formulas that made my head spin.

But here's the problem—I was *good* at it. So good, in fact, that I developed my own data tools and streamlined the process. My efficiency caught the attention of senior leadership, who decided I should take on pay planning for the entire Americas business segment. That meant leading the process for thousands of additional employees, on top of my already full workload.

I hated every minute of it. It was tedious, stressful and completely misaligned with what actually brought me joy in my job. But because I was skilled at it, everyone assumed I *wanted* to do it. At the end of the year, I was even given a company award—an actual marble obelisk to display on my desk—for my efforts. While others saw it as recognition, I saw it as a life sentence. I was now *the* pay planning person. That was my brand, whether I wanted it or not.

It's a strange paradox—many of us become known for our skills in areas we don't actually enjoy. We excel at certain tasks, perform them well and, because of that, we get asked to do them over and over again. The more we say yes, the more ingrained those tasks become in our lives, even if they bring no real satisfaction. Over time, we build entire careers, roles or responsibilities around things we never actively chose—simply because we were competent at them.

This is where the cycle of obligation takes hold. When we do something well, people assume we *like* doing it. And in some cases, we're even rewarded for it—praise, promotions, recognition, a reputation as the "go-to" person for a certain skill. But when that skill isn't aligned with what we actually *like*, all of that external reinforcement becomes a trap rather than a reward. The more we deliver, the harder it is to step away and before we know it, we're stuck in a loop of performing tasks that drain us rather than fulfill us.

I call this the *no good deed goes unpunished* phenomenon. Maybe you did a fantastic job organizing last year's family reunion, but the whole experience made you miserable. This year, when planning time rolls around, guess who's expected to handle it again? You. Because you were "so good at it." Or maybe you baked an impressive cake for a team event once and now everyone assumes you *love* baking and expects you to bring the dessert every time. In the workplace, this can be even more damaging. If you're particularly good at managing spreadsheets, handling conflict or writing reports, you may find yourself constantly assigned those tasks—regardless of whether they bring you any joy.

This cycle can be exhausting and it's easy to lose sight of the fact that being good at something doesn't mean we *must* keep doing it. If we don't set boundaries and make conscious choices, we can easily spend our days stuck in our zones of competence and excellence, rather than stepping into the work that truly lights us up. The challenge, then, is recognizing when we're in this pattern and beginning to ask a different question—not *Am I good at this?* but *Do I want to keep doing this?*

My experience with pay planning was a wake-up call. I realized that if I didn't actively choose the work I wanted to be known for, other people would choose for me. And they wouldn't necessarily choose based on what sparked joy for me—they would choose based on what was most convenient or useful for them. That's the danger of letting proficiency dictate our path instead of passion.

True alignment requires intentionality. It means being deliberate about the tasks, projects and responsibilities we take on—not just because we can do them, but because we *want* to. It means stepping back and asking, *Am I saying yes because this excites me? Or am I saying yes because it's expected?* The more we practice choosing joy over obligation, the more we steer our lives in a direction that truly fits who we are.

THE CORPORATE TRAP

There's a particular frustration that comes with being recognized for something you don't actually enjoy. When I was excelling at pay planning in corporate HR, the recognition didn't feel like an achievement—it felt like a trap. I had poured time and effort into making the process more efficient, but instead of that being a one-time success, it cemented my role in something I had no desire to keep doing. The praise and awards didn't bring fulfillment; they reinforced my misalignment. I felt dread every time I looked at that obelisk award.

Being skilled at something doesn't mean it's what you're meant to do. Yet, when we're competent—especially if we're *exceptional* at a task—it can become our defining trait in the eyes of others. It's how people categorize us, how they assign us work and how they justify giving us more of the same, whether or not it aligns with what we actually want. And the more we succeed, the harder it becomes to step away, because the external validation can feel like proof that we *should* stay in that role.

True alignment comes when we operate in the space where our skills, joy and purpose intersect. This is where work feels both meaningful and effortless, where we're energized instead of drained and where we could lose hours happily immersed in what we're doing. Recognizing the difference between excellence and genius is key to breaking free from misaligned success. The challenge isn't just knowing what we're good at—it's choosing to pursue what truly lights us up.

THE FOUR ZONES OF PERFORMANCE: UNDERSTANDING WHERE YOU OPERATE

One of the biggest challenges in creating a life that feels aligned and fulfilling is understanding where we spend our time and energy. Too often, we focus on what we *can* do rather than what we *love* to do. We take on tasks out of obligation, habit or external expectations, rather than intentional choice.

Gay Hendricks, in *The Big Leap*, introduces a powerful framework that breaks our work and activities into four zones: **the Zone of Incompetence, the Zone of Competence, the Zone of Excellence** and **the Zone of Genius.** These categories help us assess not just our skill level but our level of enjoyment and fulfillment. Understanding where we operate within these zones allows us to make strategic decisions about how we spend our time—and how we can shift toward our most fulfilling work.

ZONE 1: THE ZONE OF INCOMPETENCE

These are tasks that you *neither enjoy nor excel at.* They drain your energy, take longer than they should and often leave you feeling frustrated or inadequate.

Think about a time when you struggled through a task that could have been simple for someone else. Maybe it's wrestling with spreadsheets, fixing a leaky sink or trying to design a website when you have no technical background. You spend far too much time on it, you're unhappy while doing it and in the end, the results are mediocre at best. These are the tasks that make you mutter, *there has to be a better way or better person to do this.*

KEY REALIZATION:

The goal is to delegate, automate or remove as many of these tasks from your life as possible. Staying stuck in this zone means constantly battling frustration and inefficiency. If it's something you need to learn, that's one thing. But if it's something that will never be a strength, find a way to let it go.

REFLECTION QUESTIONS:
- What are the tasks you struggle with the most in your daily life or work?
- Are there recurring responsibilities that you dread because you're just not good at them?
- How much time do you spend in this zone? Could you delegate, trade or eliminate any of these tasks?

ZONE 2: THE ZONE OF COMPETENCE

The next step up is the **Zone of Competence**—tasks that you *can* do and may even be relatively efficient at, but they don't excite or fulfill you. They don't require special talent or passion and someone else could likely do them just as well (or better).

This is where many people get stuck because they're **functional but not fulfilled.** You might be competent at data entry, managing logistics or writing reports, but these tasks don't bring joy or excitement. You might even do them automatically, without considering whether they actually serve your bigger goals.

This is the zone where we have to think **just because I can, doesn't mean I should.** It's easy to get weighed down with competent work that fills our schedules but doesn't move us toward true fulfillment.

KEY REALIZATION:

Just because you're capable of something doesn't mean it's the best use of your time. The more time you spend in the Zone of Competence, the more you prevent yourself from operating in the zones that bring real joy and impact.

REFLECTION QUESTIONS:

- What tasks do you do regularly that you *can* handle but don't particularly enjoy?
- Do you find yourself taking on responsibilities because you're capable, rather than because they excite you?
- Are there opportunities to outsource or shift these tasks to free up time for higher-value work? Might this task be perfect for a junior colleague looking to grow?

ZONE 3: THE ZONE OF EXCELLENCE

The **Zone of Excellence** is a deceptively comfortable place to be. This is where you *really* shine—where your skills and experience set you apart and you're often recognized, rewarded and encouraged to keep going.

On the surface, this seems like the ideal place to be. You're successful, people respect your work and you might even be paid well for it. But there's a catch: **just because you're excelling at something doesn't mean it's where you're meant to be.**

This is the zone where high achievers can easily get trapped. If you're naturally gifted at something or you've spent years developing expertise, it can be incredibly hard to walk away—even if you don't love it. Society conditions us to prioritize success over fulfillment and the Zone of Excellence is where that conditioning keeps us stuck.

People in this zone often feel an underlying sense of frustration or stagnation. They know they're capable of more, but they can't quite articulate what's missing. They may even feel guilty for wanting something different, because on paper, everything looks great.

This is exactly where I found myself with pay planning in HR. I had built a system so efficient and effective that my leaders assumed I loved it. I was given awards, recognition and new projects—all of which just locked me deeper into work that felt draining and unfulfilling. I began to cringe every time someone said, "But you're so good at it!" It took time for me to realize that just because I was exceptional at something didn't mean it was the right path for me.

KEY REALIZATION:

If you feel like you're succeeding on the outside but stagnant on the inside, you might be in your Zone of Excellence. The challenge is to recognize that you have permission to pivot toward something greater—toward work that feels effortless and fulfilling.

REFLECTION QUESTIONS:

- Are you currently excelling at something that doesn't actually light you up?
- Have you ever felt guilty for wanting more even when you're already succeeding?
- What would it look like to shift even part of your time away from your Zone of Excellence?

ZONE 4: THE ZONE OF GENIUS

The **Zone of Genius** is the holy grail—this is where your greatest strengths intersect with your deepest joy. This is the work that feels effortless, where time disappears and where you feel the most alive.

In this zone, you're not just good at something—you *love* it. You feel energized, excited and in flow. Work doesn't feel like work. You can't imagine *not* doing it. This is the space where **your unique gifts make their greatest impact.**

This doesn't mean every moment is easy or free from challenges. But even when there are obstacles, you face them with excitement rather than dread. You feel like you're doing the work you were meant to do. This was where Kyla was when she was coaching other people, even when that wasn't the focus of her actual corporate job. Helping other people find success absolutely lit her up.

This is also the hardest zone to step into, because it requires intentionality. It also requires saying no to many other opportunities. The world will always reward you for staying in your Zone of Excellence and it takes courage to pursue something that might not have an immediate external pay-off. But the long-term rewards—both personally and professionally—are immeasurable.

KEY REALIZATION:

Your Zone of Genius is where you can make the greatest impact while feeling the most fulfilled. The more time you can shift toward this space, the more aligned your life will feel.

REFLECTION QUESTIONS:

- What are the activities that make you lose track of time because you're so immersed?
- If you could design your ideal workday what tasks would be included?
- Are there elements of your Zone of Genius that you're currently overlooking or not prioritizing?

SHIFTING TOWARD YOUR ZONE OF GENIUS

Now that you understand these four zones, take an honest inventory of your life. How much time do you currently spend in each one? If you're stuck in your **Zone of Excellence**, what small shifts could you make to move toward your **Zone of Genius**? If you're drowning in your **Zone of Incompetence or Competence**, what can you delegate or let go of?

Your goal isn't to jump immediately into a life where you only do work in your Zone of Genius. That's not realistic. But if you can make incremental shifts—*one decision at a time*—you'll begin to notice a profound difference. The more time you can spend in your Zone of Genius, the more fulfillment, creativity and alignment you'll bring into your life.

This is where real transformation happens.

THE SCIENCE OF LIKES: HOW PREFERENCES REVEAL POTENTIAL TALENTS

Our personal likes aren't just random preferences—they are clues. They serve as small but significant indicators of our natural strengths, hidden talents and untapped potential. What we enjoy doing often aligns with what we have the capacity to excel at, but too often, we dismiss these likes as unimportant or unrelated to our career paths.

Instead of brushing them aside, we can reframe our likes as valuable data points. By paying attention to what consistently sparks joy, engagement or curiosity, we can start piecing together a bigger picture of what truly fulfills us. Think of your likes as a compass, subtly pointing toward areas where your strengths and passions intersect. The more you tune in, the clearer the direction becomes.

LIKES AS DATA: EXPERIMENTING WITH YOUR PREFERENCES

One of the most powerful ways to uncover our potential is to treat life as an ongoing experiment. Just like scientists gather data, test hypotheses and refine their conclusions, we can apply the same process to understanding ourselves.

Think about it: when scientists conduct research, they don't expect to find the perfect answer on the first try. They test, observe, adjust and try again. The same applies to discovering what brings us true fulfillment. We are all running our own long-term experiment—every experience, job, hobby or interest is a piece of data that helps us refine our understanding of what we truly love.

Some questions to consider as you approach life with a scientist's mindset:

- What activities make you feel energized rather than drained? (We'll do The Smiley Face Test below to help you identify these.)
- What are the things you *keep coming back to* over time?
- Where have you found flow—those moments when you lose track of time because you're so engaged?
- What have you started and *not* liked? (This data is just as valuable as identifying what you do enjoy.)

Each of these observations serves as a hypothesis test—you are gathering information about yourself through real-world experience. Rather than expecting a lightning-bolt moment of clarity, treat each step as a piece of the puzzle, helping you refine your alignment over time.

USING LIKES TO FINE-TUNE ALIGNMENT

The key to understanding your likes isn't just recognizing them—it's actively experimenting with them. This means following your curiosity, testing out different activities and seeing what feels good *in practice*, not just in theory.

For example, you might enjoy writing, but in what way? Do you love writing personal essays, storytelling, technical writing, or marketing copy? Maybe you love organizing things—but is that in the form of physical spaces, business operations or content strategies? Perhaps you enjoy coaching others but do you prefer working with individuals, groups, men in a certain age demographic, CEOs or college students? By testing different versions of what we like, we gain clarity on *how* our preferences translate into real strengths.

Once you start approaching your preferences with curiosity rather than pressure, you'll find that your likes naturally guide you toward areas where your talents and fulfillment align. It's all about continuous refinement—adjusting as you learn more about what lights you up, discarding what doesn't fit and moving closer to a life that reflects who you truly are.

THE SMILEY FACE TEST

One of the simplest yet most effective ways to gain insight into what aligns with your true self is to categorize your activities, tasks and interests based on how they make you feel. The Smiley Face Test helps bring clarity to your preferences by assigning an intuitive, emotional response to different aspects of your daily life.

Instead of overthinking what you "should" like or what you're simply good at, this exercise helps you see the patterns in what genuinely brings joy versus what drains you. *The goal is to identify what energizes you, what feels neutral and what actively depletes your enthusiasm.*

STEP 1: MAKE YOUR LIST

Grab a notebook or open a blank document. Write down a list of all the activities, tasks and responsibilities you engage in regularly—both personal and professional. This includes:

- Work tasks
- Hobbies and creative pursuits

- Household chores
- Social activities
- Volunteer work or side projects
- Any recurring responsibilities

Be as thorough as possible—this exercise works best when you don't filter or edit yourself. The goal is to get **everything** on paper before evaluating.

STEP 2: CATEGORIZE YOUR LIST

Now, go through each item and assign it one of the following smiley faces based on how it makes you feel:

- ☹ **Dislike:** These are the tasks that drain your energy, feel like a chore or create frustration.
  You might be good at them, but you dread doing them.
- 😐 **Neutral:** These are the tasks you don't necessarily mind, but they don't excite or fulfill you either. You do them out of habit, necessity or obligation.
- 😄 **Like:** These are the tasks that **light you up**. They bring joy, creativity, fulfillment or a sense of purpose. You find yourself energized when doing them.

STEP 3: ANALYZE YOUR PATTERNS

Look at your completed list and see if you notice any themes.

Ask yourself:

- What do the "likes" have in common? Are they creative, social, structured, independent?
- Are there any surprises in your "dislike" category?
- Do your work responsibilities mostly fall into the "neutral" category? If so, what does that reveal about your level of engagement?
- Are there tasks you've placed in the "like" column that you're not currently making time for?
- Do you see any connections between your "likes" and the strengths you've identified in previous exercises?

STEP 4: MAKE SMALL SHIFTS TOWARD ALIGNMENT

Now that you have a clearer picture of what energizes you versus what drains you, set an intention to adjust your time and energy accordingly:

- **Increase Your Time on 😄 Activities:** Look for ways to do more of what you enjoy. Can you prioritize these tasks at work? Can you integrate them into your daily routine?

- **Delegate or Reduce ☹ Tasks:** If something consistently drains you, is there a way to delegate, automate or minimize your involvement? Sometimes, a small shift in approach can make a huge difference.

- **Re-evaluate Your 😐 Tasks:** For things that fall into the neutral zone, consider whether they are necessary or if they can be adjusted to bring more enjoyment. Can you make them more engaging, collaborate with others or tie them to a greater purpose?

WHY THIS WORKS

This exercise allows you to **visually see** where your energy is going. It helps cut through the mental noise of "what should I be doing?" and focuses on what actually feels right. Over time, small shifts toward your activities and away from tasks create a more aligned, fulfilling life.

By recognizing what brings you joy and actively pursuing more of it, you begin moving toward a life and career that naturally supports your strengths and values. This isn't about making an overnight transformation—it's about making small, intentional choices that bring you closer to alignment every day.

REMEMBER THIS

Identifying what you like isn't just about picking hobbies or making a feel-good list—it's about **understanding what energizes you, what fulfills you and what truly aligns with who you are at your core**. Your likes hold powerful clues about the work, relationships and activities that will bring you the most satisfaction in life. They help illuminate your **Zone of Genius**— the space where your strengths and joy intersect.

But here's the key: this isn't a one-time exercise. Life evolves and so do you. The things you like now may shift over time as you grow, explore new experiences and refine your sense of purpose. That's why it's crucial to revisit your list regularly—treat it as a living guide that helps steer you toward choices that feel right.

YOUR NEXT STEPS

1. **Review Your List Often** – When making career decisions, taking on new commitments or setting goals, use your list as a reference point. Does this opportunity align with what you genuinely enjoy?

2. **Make Small, Intentional Shifts** – Start integrating more of your "likes" into your daily routine while gradually stepping away from tasks that drain you.

3. **Trust Your Preferences** – Your likes are not random. They are signals guiding you toward fulfillment. Give yourself permission to prioritize them.

Every small choice you make in favor of your true preferences is a step closer to a life that is not just successful on paper but genuinely aligned with your joy and purpose. The more you shape your life around what you love, the more you unlock your fullest potential.

So, what will you choose today? 🔑

CHAPTER SEVEN

Key: Indicators

IN THE LAST chapter, we explored the importance of identifying what we like—the activities, tasks and experiences that bring us joy, energy and a sense of fulfillment. But there's another side to that equation, one that is just as critical to alignment: knowing what we don't like. If pinpointing our likes helps us move toward a life of purpose and fulfillment, then understanding our dislikes ensures we don't waste time and energy in the wrong places.

We often assume that the key to a happy life is simply doing more of what we enjoy. And while that's true, it's only part of the picture. The other half—the often-overlooked half—is actively removing what drains us, frustrates us or pulls us further from alignment. Because here's the thing: it doesn't matter how much you love one aspect of your life if another part is quietly (or loudly) eroding your well-being. You can be in a great relationship, but if you're stuck in a soul-sucking job, your days will still feel heavy. You can enjoy your work but if you're constantly obligated to social commitments you secretly dread, your energy will still be depleted.

So much of personal misalignment comes from tolerating or forcing ourselves into situations that don't fit us. We convince ourselves that we should be grateful for opportunities that, in reality, drain us. We rationalize the discomfort by telling ourselves, *this is just how life is*, or *I don't have a choice*. We say yes to responsibilities we have no interest in because we don't want to disappoint others. Over time, all of these small compromises add up and suddenly, we find ourselves exhausted, stuck and resentful without really understanding how we got there.

This chapter is about bringing awareness to those misaligned areas. It's about listening to the discomfort, not as something to be ignored or pushed through but as valuable data—a flashing indicator light warning you that something is off. Because the truth is, sometimes the most productive thing we can do isn't adding more of what we love; it's subtracting what we don't.

THE QUARTER-LIFE CRISIS: A WAKE-UP CALL

Looking back, I can see the warning signs so clearly. At the time, though, I felt completely trapped—spinning inside what I now call *the vortex*. It wasn't just one thing that was wrong; it was *everything* or at least that's how it felt. My job was a daily battle against a toxic boss who thrived on tearing me down.

My marriage, which had felt like the natural next step when I was young and eager to move forward in life, was shifting in ways I couldn't fully articulate. Financial stress loomed over us, made worse by the weight of student loans I had co-signed for my then-husband, a decision that would haunt me long after the marriage ended. And then, because apparently, I wasn't overwhelmed enough, we decided to buy a house—an old, charming, money-pit of a house—without any real plan, guidance or understanding of what that would entail.

The stress of it all was suffocating. I woke up every day with a sense of dread so heavy that it felt like my body was resisting consciousness. I was constantly in motion—working, commuting, dealing with home repairs, trying to meet expectations at work and at home—but I wasn't actually *going* anywhere. I was existing, reacting, surviving. I thought I was handling it because that's what I had always done: *push through, keep going, don't complain.* That's the mindset I had been raised with and it had served me well in school and early in my career. But in real life? In a deeply misaligned life? It was the very thing keeping me stuck.

At the time, I didn't have the language to articulate what was happening. I didn't recognize the signs of burnout, anxiety or depression. All I knew was that I wanted out. I fantasized about getting in my car, pointing it in the opposite direction of everything and just driving—no destination, no plan, just *away*. Some days, I caught myself thinking that if I got in a minor accident—nothing too serious, just enough to land me in the hospital for a little while—I could finally get a break. Those thoughts terrified me, but I didn't know what to do with them. I didn't know who to call. I couldn't imagine anyone else having had experience with these feelings and I felt ashamed to have them. So I kept going.

These are what I now recognize as **indicator feelings**—those gut-level emotions that tell us something is deeply misaligned. Overwhelm, anxiety, dread, resentment—these aren't just unpleasant emotions to push through; they're signals, like flashing warning lights on a dashboard, alerting us that something is wrong. But I wasn't listening. Instead, I did what so many of us do: I tried to *outwork* my unhappiness, convincing myself that if I just kept checking the boxes—if I kept achieving, producing, meeting expectations—then surely things would get better.

Spoiler: they didn't. Because misalignment doesn't resolve itself. It demands attention. It demands change. Just like those dashboard lights on your car that don't magically resolve over time. And eventually, when I couldn't hold it all together anymore, everything started to unravel. What I thought was a total collapse turned out to be my wake-up call. The question was—would I finally listen?

RECOGNIZING INDICATOR FEELINGS

We often think of emotions like frustration, exhaustion or anxiety as problems to be solved—something to push through, numb or ignore until they go away. But what if, instead, we treated them as messengers? *Indicator feelings* are exactly that: internal warning signs that something in our life isn't aligned with our well-being. They're like flashing lights on the dashboard of a car—signals designed to get our attention before the engine completely breaks down.

One of the most common indicator feelings is *dread*—that sinking sensation in your stomach when you think about a certain task, person or environment. Maybe it's the moment your alarm goes off on a workday or the way your chest tightens before a meeting with a particular colleague. Maybe it's the "Sunday Scaries" feeling that happens on the weekend when you think about facing work on Monday morning. If the mere thought of something makes you feel drained before you even start, that's not just a bad mood—it's a sign that this thing, whatever it is, is not serving you.

Apathy and exhaustion are also key indicators. If you used to care about your work but now find yourself completely indifferent, if you struggle to muster energy for even small tasks or if everything in your day feels like a chore, that's not *laziness*—it's a symptom of being disconnected from what energizes and fulfills you. When alignment is missing, motivation often vanishes right alongside it.

For many people, anxiety and physical symptoms are the body's way of waving a red flag. Frequent headaches, stomach issues, tension in your shoulders—your body often knows something is wrong before your mind fully catches up. Chronic stress and misalignment don't just impact our mental state; they take a devastating toll on our physical health too.

And then there's the big one: the desire to escape. Fantasizing about quitting your job on the spot, moving to a new city where no one knows you or walking away from responsibilities altogether—these thoughts aren't just daydreams; they're signals of deep dissatisfaction. When I was in my own quarter-life crisis, I didn't realize that my fantasies of getting in the car and driving *anywhere but here* were actually my subconscious screaming, *This isn't working. Something has to change.*

The key isn't to ignore these feelings or shame yourself for having them—it's to listen to them. They are telling you something important. Instead of brushing them off, get curious. Ask yourself: *What is this feeling trying to tell me? What isn't working? Where do I feel stuck?* These questions don't always have immediate answers but acknowledging the signals is the first step toward figuring out what needs to change.

REFLECTION EXERCISE:
IDENTIFYING YOUR INDICATOR FEELINGS

Understanding your indicator feelings starts with recognizing the specific moments and situations that trigger them. This exercise will help you pinpoint patterns in your emotional responses so you can begin making more intentional choices about where you invest your time and energy.

STEP 1: WRITE DOWN SITUATIONS THAT DRAIN YOU
Think about the moments in your day, week, or life that consistently make you feel exhausted, frustrated or overwhelmed. These can be big things, like your job or a toxic relationship or small things, like a particular weekly meeting that always puts you in a bad mood. Consider:

- What activities do you dread?
- Who drains your energy?
- What commitments feel like a burden rather than something you *want* to do?
- When do you feel trapped, uninspired or deeply unmotivated?
- Write down at least five situations, but don't overthink them—go with what immediately comes to mind.

STEP 2: IDENTIFY THE EMOTIONS TIED TO THOSE SITUATIONS

Next to each situation, write the emotion it triggers in you. Some common ones include:

- **Dread** ("I feel sick just thinking about this.")
- **Resentment** ("Why am I the one always having to do this?")
- **Exhaustion** ("I feel completely drained afterward.")
- **Apathy** ("I just don't care about this at all.")
- **Anxiety** ("My heart races whenever I have to deal with this.")
- **Irritability** ("Even the smallest thing about this makes me snap.")

If you're not sure, close your eyes and imagine the situation playing out in real time—what's your body's first reaction? Do your shoulders tense? Does your stomach drop? Does your breathing change? Often, our physical responses reveal emotions we haven't fully acknowledged.

STEP 3: TEMPORARY DISCOMFORT OR DEEPER MISALIGNMENT?

Now, take a step back and evaluate each situation. Ask yourself:

- Is this a temporary discomfort or is this a long-term issue?

- If I removed this from my life would I feel immediate relief?
- Is this something I can change or is it something I need to learn to manage differently?
- Is this misalignment affecting other areas of my life?

If a situation causes momentary discomfort but serves a meaningful purpose (like studying for a big test or preparing for a job interview), it may just be part of the process and can be reframed in context. But if it's something that brings **ongoing** stress, dread or disengagement, it could be a deeper signal that you need a change.

TAKING ACTION

After reviewing your list, circle **one** situation or emotion that stands out the most. Ask yourself:

- What's one small action I could take to improve this situation?
- Do I need to set a boundary, say no or reconsider my involvement?
- If I could remove this from my life what would change?

This isn't about fixing everything overnight—it's about recognizing what's draining you and starting to take steps toward a life that feels more aligned. Your indicator feelings are there to help guide you; all you have to do is listen.

THE COST OF IGNORING THE RED FLAGS

Ignoring what we don't like doesn't make it go away—it makes it grow. When we repeatedly push aside discomfort, rationalizing that "this is just how life is," we trap ourselves in cycles of stress, dissatisfaction and burnout. The things we tolerate become the foundation for a life we never intended to build.

THE SLOW BURN OF MISALIGNMENT

When we consistently force ourselves to endure situations that drain us, the impact goes beyond momentary frustration. Over time, ignored misalignment turns into resentment, exhaustion and disconnection from ourselves. It can manifest in different ways:

- **Emotional burnout** – Feeling perpetually exhausted, unmotivated or emotionally detached from work, relationships or personal goals.

- **Chronic stress responses** – Physical symptoms like headaches, stomach issues, insomnia or a weakened immune system. The body often knows what the mind refuses to acknowledge.

- **Loss of passion and creativity** – Struggling to find joy in activities that once felt fulfilling because mental and emotional energy is constantly being drained elsewhere.

- **Cynicism and resentment** – A growing frustration toward work, family or social commitments, feeling trapped in obligations rather than making choices from a place of purpose.

For many, this slow burn is insidious—it doesn't happen overnight, so we don't always recognize when we've slipped into survival mode. Instead, we normalize the discomfort, telling ourselves that "this is just how work is," "everyone feels like this," or "this is the price of success."

THE DANGER OF RATIONALIZING DISCOMFORT

One of the most common ways we stay stuck in misalignment is by rationalizing why we *should* tolerate things that feel wrong. We tell ourselves:

- **"This is just how it is."** (It's not. Just because something is common doesn't mean it's healthy or right for you.)

- **"I should be grateful."** (You can be grateful and still want more for yourself. These two things are not mutually exclusive.)

- **"Everyone else is dealing with the same thing."** (What works for others doesn't mean it's the right path for you.)

- **"I don't have any other options."** (There are always options—some may be difficult, but they exist.)

- **"If I just push through, it will get better."** (Sometimes perseverance pays off but other times it just prolongs suffering.)

We convince ourselves that discomfort is an inevitable part of life, which, to an extent, is true—life will always have challenges. But there's a difference between temporary discomfort that leads to growth and ongoing misalignment that leads to burnout.

RECOGNIZING WHEN IT'S TIME TO MAKE A CHANGE

The key is learning to distinguish between a challenge to overcome and a fundamental misalignment.

If something is **stretching you in a way that helps you grow** (learning a new skill, working toward a meaningful but difficult goal), then the discomfort may be a necessary part of the process.

But if something is **consistently draining you without any sense of fulfillment or progress**, it's a red flag that something needs to change.

Alignment isn't about avoiding all discomfort—it's about knowing when discomfort is a sign to keep going and when it's a sign to walk away. Your discomfort isn't always an obstacle to push through. Sometimes, it's a signal pointing you toward something better.

NAVIGATING TOXICITY IN WORK AND RELATIONSHIPS

Early in my career, I worked for a toxic boss—the kind of person who thrived on manipulation, rumor-spreading and outright hostility. She was a woman with power, many years my senior and she made it her mission to make my life miserable. I don't know why. She spread vicious rumors about me, including an entirely fabricated affair with a married man in another department—someone I barely knew. The absurdity of it was almost laughable, except that it wasn't. It was calculated. It was malicious. And worst of all, it worked.

I was 26, brand new to the company and completely unequipped to deal with someone like her. She wasn't just my boss; she was the Vice President of HR and the General Counsel. There was no one to turn to. I felt trapped, completely powerless to stop the damage she was inflicting on my reputation and my confidence. Every single day was a battlefield and no matter how hard I tried to keep my head down, the hostility seeped into everything.

THE EMOTIONAL TOLL OF TOXICITY

At the time, I didn't have the language for what I was experiencing. I didn't recognize the gas lighting, the subtle (and not-so-subtle) ways she undermined me. All I knew was that I dreaded going to work. I carried that tension in my body— my stomach was constantly in knots, my shoulders ached from being perpetually tensed and I had trouble sleeping. I blamed myself for feeling overwhelmed, convinced that I was the problem.

I internalized the idea that this was just how work was. I told myself to tough it out, that she was hard on me because she saw potential in me, that maybe I *was* too sensitive. I con-vinced myself that if I just worked harder, if I proved myself, the situation would change. It didn't. It only got worse.

But here's what I didn't understand then:

- **Toxicity isn't just a bad day or a difficult boss**—it's a pattern of behavior that erodes your confidence, well-being and sense of self.

- **Toughing it out isn't always the right answer.** Enduring mistreatment isn't a badge of honor; it's a warning sign that something needs to change.

- **Toxicity isn't isolated.** When your work environment is toxic, it follows you home. It bleeds into your relation-ships, your health and your overall happiness.

THE FALSE BELIEF THAT TOUGHING IT OUT IS THE ANSWER

For so long, I believed that enduring this situation made me stronger. That pushing through, gritting my teeth and keep-ing my head down was the only way to succeed. I thought complaining would make me seem weak. I thought quitting would make me a failure. I thought the problem was me.

But let me say this clearly:

- **There is no prize for suffering.** Staying in a toxic situation doesn't build character; it erodes it.
- **You don't have to earn the right to leave.** You don't need to prove that it's "bad enough" before you walk away.
- **The longer you stay, the harder it is to recognize how much damage it's doing.**

Looking back, I wish someone had told me that I wasn't crazy, that my feelings were valid, that I didn't have to endure this just because I was young and early in my career. That toxic environments don't deserve your loyalty.

WHEN TOXICITY SPILLS INTO EVERYTHING

When work is toxic, it doesn't stay at work. It follows you home. It changes how you see yourself. It affects how you interact with your loved ones, how much patience you have for your partner, how much energy you have left for yourself. It warps your perception of what is *normal*.

I was carrying the weight of that job on my back every single day and I didn't even realize how heavy it was until much later. I was also dealing with a marriage that was shifting into a new season—one that neither of us was prepared for. We were young, navigating new careers, financial stress and life pressures without a solid foundation. And because I was already exhausted from work, I had nothing left to give to my personal life. The toxicity of my job seeped into my marriage, my friendships and my ability to even think clearly about what I wanted.

This is what misalignment does. It starts in one area, but if left unchecked, it spreads.

It took me years to fully understand the damage that experience did—not just to my career but to my confidence, my ability to advocate for myself and my understanding of what I deserved. It took even longer to unlearn the belief that suffering equals strength.

If you're in a toxic situation right now—whether it's at work, in a relationship or any other area of life—I want you to pay attention to how it makes you feel.

- If you dread waking up in the morning.
- If you constantly second-guess yourself.
- If you feel drained, depleted and disrespected.
- If you find yourself fantasizing about disappearing or starting over.

These are not feelings that should be normalized. These are indicator feelings. They are telling you something is wrong. And ignoring them won't make them go away—it will only make them louder.

REFLECTION EXERCISE: THE ENERGY AUDIT

One of the most powerful ways to assess alignment in your life is to take a close look at how different areas affect your energy. Some things naturally energize us, making us feel more engaged, fulfilled and alive. Others drain us, leaving us depleted, frustrated or even resentful. The Energy Audit helps bring clarity to where your energy is going and what might need to shift.

STEP 1: LIST MAJOR AREAS OF YOUR LIFE

Grab the notebook and write down the major areas of your life. Consider:

- **Work/Career** (previous roles, current role, major skill sets, certificates, degrees)
- **Relationships** (romantic, friendships, family, social circles)
- **Health** (physical, emotional, mental, spiritual well-being)
- **Finances** (income, savings, debt, expenses, financial goals)
- **Home Life** (environment, daily routines, household responsibilities)
- **Personal Growth** (hobbies, learning, creativity, self-improvement)

   Feel free to add any other categories that are relevant to your life.

STEP 2: ASSIGN AN ENERGY RATING
For each category, assign a rating from 1 to 5, based on how that area makes you feel.

- **1-2** = Completely draining. This area of life is exhausting, stressful or unfulfilling.
- **3** = Neutral. It's not terrible, but it doesn't energize you either. It just *exists*.
- **4-5** = Energizing. This area of life excites, fulfills or deeply satisfies you.

Be brutally honest with yourself—there are no wrong answers here. The goal is to get a clear picture of how each area impacts your overall well-being.

STEP 3: IDENTIFY PATTERNS & WHAT NEEDS TO CHANGE
Now, take a step back and look at your ratings.

- **Where is your biggest drain coming from?**
  Any categories scoring a **1-2** should be red flags—these are areas of misalignment that might need urgent attention.

- **What areas feel neutral (3), and why?** Is there room for improvement? Can you make small adjustments to increase fulfillment?

- **Where do you feel energized (4-5), and how can you do more of what lights you up?**

If your life feels heavily weighted toward the draining end of the scale, it's time to consider some shifts. Maybe it's a toxic work environment, an unbalanced relationship or an obligation that you've outgrown. Where is misalignment stealing your energy?

This exercise isn't about instant fixes—it's about awareness. When you clearly see what's draining and fueling you, you can start making intentional choices that bring you closer to alignment. Small changes lead to big shifts over time.

Now, take a moment to reflect:

- What surprised you most about your energy audit?
- What is one small change you can make today to bring your energy balance closer to where you want it to be?

Start there. Your energy is one of your most valuable resources—spend it wisely.

THE PRESSURE TO FOLLOW
"THE RIGHT PATH"

One of the easiest ways to veer off course in life is by following the path we think we're supposed to take rather than the one that genuinely aligns with who we are. From an early age, we're surrounded by messages about what success is supposed to look like—go to school, get a good job, settle down, buy a house and stay the course. These expectations come from well meaning family members, societal norms and cultural traditions, but they often fail to consider who we actually are and what we truly want.

For many people, major life decisions—where to live, what career to pursue, when to start a family—are shaped less by personal passion and more by a desire to meet external expectations. We absorb these pressures as absolute truths, rarely pausing to ask: *Is this even right for me?* And the more we move forward on autopilot, the harder it becomes to recognize when we've drifted away from alignment.

WHEN "SHOULDS" OVERRIDE WHAT'S RIGHT

Buying my first home was a perfect example of this. At the time, I was in my mid-twenties, married and navigating a demanding job. Everything around me—family, friends, the broader societal narrative—implied that homeownership was the next logical step. Renting was seen as "throwing money away," and people around me made it seem like we were making a terrible mistake by not getting into the real estate market.

I didn't question it. I didn't pause to ask if buying a house was the right choice for us at that time in our lives. Instead, I did what seemed like the *responsible* thing, what was expected. Without much preparation or research, we dove into the home-buying process, guided by nothing more than the belief that "this is what adults do."

What followed was a series of costly and exhausting missteps—choosing a house that needed far more work than we could handle, taking on a mortgage that stretched us financially and locking ourselves into a location that made my already stressful job even worse. Every day, the weight of this decision pressed down harder, making me realize that what's considered the "right path" isn't always right for you.

THE CONSEQUENCES OF RUSHING INTO MISALIGNMENT

This experience taught me a hard lesson: external voices do not have to dictate your choices. When we rush into major commitments—whether it's a home, a job, a relationship—without truly evaluating if they align with our needs and desires, we set ourselves up for stress, frustration and even regret.

The problem is, these pressures don't just disappear once the decision is made. The more we force ourselves into misaligned choices, the more we feel trapped—trapped by financial obligations, by fear of change, by the belief that we can't walk away because we've already invested so much.

But here's the truth: You don't have to stay stuck in something just because it was once considered a good idea. And you don't have to accept every "should" that comes your way. What's considered the right path for others may be completely wrong for you.

REWRITING THE NARRATIVE

If there's one takeaway from this experience, it's this: pause before making big life decisions.

Give yourself permission to ask:

- Do I actually want this?
- Am I making this choice for myself or because it's expected of me?
- What would happen if I gave myself more time to decide?

There's no deadline on building a life that aligns with you. The world will always be full of opinions about what you *should* do, but you are the only one who has to live with the decisions you make.

WHEN IGNORING DISCOMFORT TURNS DANGEROUS

There's a certain point where misalignment stops being an inconvenience and starts becoming something much more insidious. The longer we force ourselves to endure situations that drain us—whether it's a toxic job, an unhealthy relationship or a life structure that doesn't fit—the more it chips away at our well-being.

Sometimes, the signs are subtle at first. A Sunday night sense of dread before the workweek. A feeling of exhaustion that sleep doesn't fix. An edge of resentment toward obligations that once seemed manageable. But if we ignore these warning signs, they can escalate into something far more serious: depression, anxiety and the quiet, creeping thought that maybe there's no way out.

I didn't recognize how bad things had gotten until I started having fantasies about getting into a car accident. Not a catastrophic one, but one just bad enough that I'd have to be in the hospital for a while—long enough to press pause on everything and simply get a break. I wasn't actively suicidal, but looking back, I can see how dangerously close my mind was to waving a white flag. I wanted an external force to pull me out of my situation because I felt like I had no other options. I felt powerless to make any changes.

That kind of thinking doesn't happen overnight. It's the result of months or years of ignoring discomfort, pushing through exhaustion and believing that you *have* to keep going, no matter how miserable you are. The scary part is that this kind of slow, creeping burnout is easy to rationalize. I told myself that this was just how life worked. That I was supposed to be stressed. That my job, my marriage, my obligations— none of it was *that* bad, so why was I complaining?

It wasn't until much later that I realized this truth: Thoughts of escape—whether it's disappearing, starting over or even fantasizing about getting hurt—are not OK for you to normalize. They're a red flag. If you've ever caught yourself daydreaming about vanishing from your own life, it's not because you're broken. It's because something is deeply misaligned, and your mind is trying to find a way out.

SEEKING HELP IS A SIGN OF STRENGTH, NOT FAILURE

One of the hardest things to accept when you're in the depths of misalignment is that it's okay to ask for help. I didn't grow up in an environment where people talked about mental health. I thought struggling meant I was weak. That I should be able to figure it out on my own. That everyone else seemed to be managing just fine, so why couldn't I?

I wish I had known then what I know now: You don't have to wait until you're at rock bottom to reach out. Finding the right therapist, coach, mentor or even just talking to someone who understands can be life-changing. If I had sought support sooner, I might have seen my situation more clearly, instead of feeling trapped inside it.

If you're reading this and recognizing yourself in these words—if you've been pushing down that nagging sense of *I can't do this anymore*—please know that you are not alone. And you are not failing. You are receiving a message, loud and clear, that something in your life needs to change. The real failure would be ignoring it.

REFLECTION EXERCISE: REWRITING THE RULES

We often stay stuck in misalignment because of unquestioned beliefs—things we've absorbed from family, society or past experiences that we've never truly examined. This exercise is designed to help you challenge the "rules" keeping you trapped and start seeing new possibilities.

STEP 1: IDENTIFY A SITUATION WHERE YOU FEEL STUCK
Think about an area of your life where you feel trapped, unfulfilled or obligated to stay in a situation that no longer serves
you. This could be a job, a relationship, a responsibility or even
a self-imposed expectation.

- "I feel like I have to stay in my current career, even
  though I hate it."
- "I always say yes to commitments I don't actually want
  to do."
- "I feel pressured to follow a life path that doesn't feel
  right for me."
- "I'm so over bringing the snacks to every school and
  youth sports event!"

**STEP 2: WRITE DOWN THE UNDERLYING BELIEF KEEPING
YOU THERE**
Now, identify the belief that's holding you in place. These often
sound logical but are actually based on fear, societal pressure
or outdated expectations.

- "I can't leave this job because it's stable."
- "I'll never find another good job if I leave this one."
- "If I say no, people will think I'm selfish."
- "I should be grateful for what I have and not want
  more."

STEP 3: CHALLENGE THAT BELIEF

Ask yourself: *Is this actually true, or is this just a story I've been told?* What would happen if I stopped believing this?

- Is stability worth sacrificing my well-being?
- Would the right people in my life still respect me if I said no?
- What if wanting more isn't selfish, but necessary for my growth?

By rewriting these internal narratives, you open up the possibility for new choices, new paths and a life that doesn't feel like a cage. Because the truth is, you don't have to wait for an accident or a crisis to give yourself permission to change. You can start right now.

My uncle likes to repeat the saying, "Those that mind don't matter and those that matter don't mind." I like keeping that in my head when wondering if I'm making a choice that I think other people might not like. I've also been exploring the concept of not being responsible for other people's feelings. Think you might disappoint your father if you change jobs? You very well might but that's his issue to process, not yours. Your job isn't to be the court jester keeping everyone else smiling and laughing.

MOVING FORWARD: WHAT DON'T YOU LIKE?

Identifying what you don't like isn't about dwelling on negativity—it's about clarity. When you understand what drains you, frustrates you or makes you feel out of sync, you gain the power to set boundaries and protect your well-being.

You have permission to let go of the things that no longer serve you. Just because something once felt like the "right" path doesn't mean you have to stay on it. Life is fluid and so are you. Growth means recognizing when it's time to pivot.

Start small. Say no to one obligation that exhausts you. Delegate a task that doesn't align with your strengths. Shift your focus, even in small ways, toward what energizes you instead of what depletes you. Each step away from misalignment is a step closer to a life that truly fits.

Things I've stopped doing or said no to:

- Serving as a board member for a nonprofit that started out fulfilling but, over time, turned into hours and hours of unpaid work. It's OK to stop. It is not your responsibility to solve another organization's staffing or workload issues.

- Feeling like I needed to participate in "extracurricular activities" as an adult only because they looked good on my resume. I'm an adult in my 50's, I don't need to prove that I'm a worthy human.

- Thinking I owed people an explanation when I said no. "You're right Karen, I wasn't at church last week." Full stop.

And guess what? It feels so good. 🔑

CHAPTER EIGHT

Key: Thoughts, Feelings & Behaviors

I REMEMBER THE exact moment I realized something was wrong. Not wrong like "oops, I made a mistake," but wrong in that way where something inside you quietly whispers: *You're not okay.*

A dear friend had driven in to spend the weekend. The kind of friend who knows your coffee order and your childhood crush and who shows up with journals and cute pens because she knows how much you love a good reflection activity. She'd put together a little ritual for us—something cozy and inspiring to start the new year. We lit candles, poured tea and curled up on the couch with our notebooks.

The first journal prompt was simple enough: *Write down some specific moments of joy from this year.*

I stared at the page.

Nothing came.

I scanned through months in my head—family dinners, travel, holidays, milestones, client wins, house projects, birthdays—and still... nothing. I could remember events. I could tell you what *happened*. But I couldn't *feel* any of it.

I kept waiting for the warm, bubbly feeling of joy to rise up—like it always used to. But it didn't. There was just... static. A low, persistent hum of numbness.

And that's when it hit me. I'd become so emotionally and physically tapped out that I couldn't access one memory of feeling joyful from an entire year of my life. Not because my life was empty. Far from it. On paper, things looked good—great, even. I had a thriving business, a lovely home, healthy kids, friendships, a partner, all the "success" markers that are supposed to fill us up. And yet, I felt hollow. Like I was walking through my life behind a sheet of glass.

I remember feeling embarrassed. I didn't want to say it out loud. Didn't want to disappoint my friend or admit that the girl who's always leading, planning, coaching, creating—*felt nothing*. I was afraid she'd think I was broken.

But the truth is, I was just overwhelmed. Deeply, dangerously overwhelmed. So much so that my brain and body had gone into energy conservation mode. I wasn't sad, exactly—I was *disconnected*. My nervous system had decided it couldn't process any more, and it shut the door on everything. Even joy.

That moment with the journal was a wake-up call. It was the first time I realized that emotional numbness *isn't neutral*. It's not "I'm fine." It's "something is really off." It's a blinking red light on the dashboard that we so often ignore because everything *looks* okay.

This is what emotional misalignment looks like. And this is why we have to learn to read our inner signals before we miss the turnoff completely.

That day with the journal stayed with me—not because I was embarrassed (though I was), but because it was the first time I really understood something critical: *my emotional experience wasn't matching my actual life*. And that mismatch was the clue. It wasn't that I had nothing to be joyful about. It's that I was so overloaded, so disconnected from myself, I couldn't feel it.

Which brings us to something I wish I'd known years earlier:

You are not your thoughts.

You are not your feelings.

You are the one *noticing* them.

But—and this is the part no one tells you—just because they're not *you* doesn't mean they're meaningless. In fact, they're often trying to tell you something important. Thoughts and feelings are messengers. Signals. They're little red flags or yellow lights or tugging sensations that ask us to pause and pay attention. Not to spiral, not to shame ourselves—but to *listen*.

We've been taught to push through. To stay rational. To ignore the noise in our heads or the ache in our chests and just "get it done." But what if those thoughts weren't the enemy? What if the anxiety, the irritation, the flat-out numbness were actually *clues*? Little breadcrumb trails trying to lead us back to alignment.

In this chapter, we're going to learn how to hear those messages. Not to believe every thought or obey every feeling—but to decode them. To understand the difference between *being* anxious and *feeling* anxious. To notice when a behavior is out of character and ask why, instead of judging it.

Because that's where the power lives—not in avoiding discomfort, but in getting curious about what it's trying to tell us.

REFRAMING EMOTIONS AS DATA

Somewhere along the way, many of us absorbed the message that feelings are liabilities. That they cloud judgment. That they should be compartmentalized, pushed down or silenced until it's more "convenient" to deal with them—if ever. We're praised for being composed, for having a stiff upper lip, for powering through without flinching. And if we do break down or admit we're struggling, we're often quick to apologize for it. As if being human is something to be embarrassed about.

But here's the truth: emotions aren't flaws. They're not personal defects or signs that we're failing at adulting. They're data.

Emotions are internal indicators—like the lights on your car dashboard—that flash not because you're broken, but because something needs attention. That feeling of dread on Sunday night? That tightness in your chest during a meeting? That burst of energy when you're finally working on something you care about? All of that is data. It's valuable. It's your internal compass trying to point you toward—or away from—something.

There's a phrase I come back to often, especially when I find myself shoving uncomfortable emotions aside: *What we resist, persists.* And it's true. The more we try to ignore or suppress a feeling, the more it builds pressure behind the scenes. Eventually, it spills out sideways—through exhaustion, resentment, snapping at people we love or numbing ourselves just to get through the day. The feeling doesn't go away. It just gets louder.

This chapter isn't about letting emotions take over the wheel and drive the car off the road. It's about learning to read the dashboard before we end up in the ditch. It's about practicing the skill of noticing—without panic, without judgment—and asking, "What is this feeling trying to show me?"

You don't have to obey every feeling. But what if you let them speak before you shut the door on them?

Let's start listening.

THE COGNITIVE TRIANGLE:
THOUGHTS, FEELINGS, BEHAVIORS

One of the most helpful frameworks I've ever come across for understanding what's really going on beneath the surface is something called the **Cognitive Triangle**. If you've ever been in therapy, especially with someone who practices cognitive behavioral therapy (CBT), you've probably seen some version of this. It's simple, it's powerful and once you see how it works, you can't *unsee* it.

Here's the idea: our **thoughts**, **feelings** and **behaviors** are all connected—and they influence one another in a continuous loop.

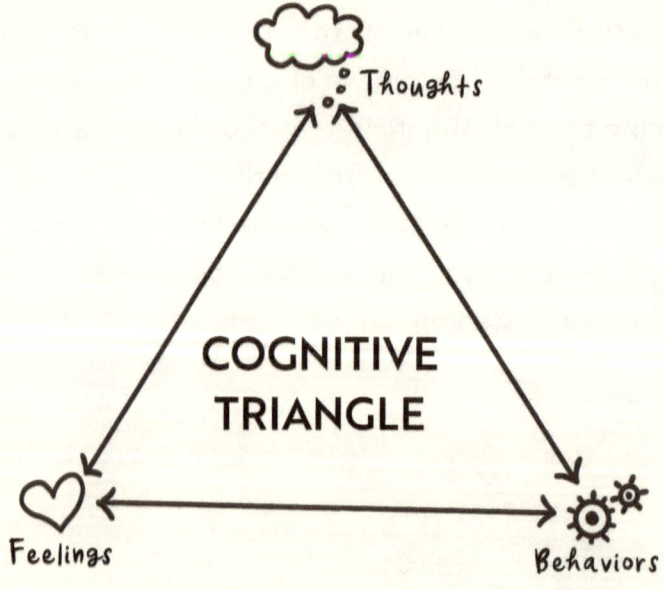

Let's break it down:

THOUGHTS

These are the interpretations and internal stories we create about what's happening around us. They can be words, images, assumptions, memories or mental commentaries that flash through our brains—often without us even realizing it. Thoughts sound like:

- "I'm so far behind."
- "She's mad at me."
- "I should have handled that better."
- "I'll never get this right."

The tricky thing is, we tend to accept these thoughts as *truth*—even when they're not. And because our brains are wired to be efficient, the more we think a certain way, the more automatic those thoughts become.

FEELINGS

Feelings are our body's physiological and emotional responses to those thoughts. This is where our nervous system kicks in. Your thoughts trigger a feeling—sometimes subtle, sometimes full-on thunderstorm. Think:

- Butterflies in your stomach
- A knot in your throat

- A racing heart
- The weight of sadness in your chest
- The heat of anger rising in your face

These sensations aren't random. They're your body's way of responding to the story your brain is telling.

BEHAVIORS

Then comes what we *do* (or don't do) as a result. These are our actions, habits, reactions and choices—many of which happen on autopilot. For example:

- You avoid having a difficult conversation because you *feel* anxious, which came from the *thought* "They'll be upset with me."
- Or you overwork to prove your worth because you *feel* insecure, driven by the *thought* "I'm not doing enough."

Behavior is often the place where misalignment becomes visible. It's where burnout, avoidance, resentment and stuck show up. But it's also the place where we can create real, lasting change.

Here's the good news: **change any one part of the triangle and you influence the other two.** If you can interrupt an unhelpful thought and reframe it, your feelings shift—and so does your behavior.

If you take a small, healthy action (even when you don't feel like it), your brain takes note—and your thoughts and emotions start to realign. This is what gives us agency. We don't have to wait until everything feels perfect. We just have to start paying attention and choosing one small entry point into the loop.

Coming up next, I'll show you what this looks like in real life—and how learning to notice your thoughts, feelings and behaviors can be the beginning of a radically different experience.

REAL TALK: WHAT AUTOMATIC THOUGHTS SOUND LIKE

Let's get honest about the running commentary in our heads. You know the one. It's that little whisper—or sometimes full-blown shout—that says things like:

- "I'm so behind. I'll never catch up."
- "Everyone else is better at this than I am."
- "I'm not good at this. I'm probably going to mess it up."
- "I should be more productive."
- "That was such a dumb thing to say."
- "What's wrong with me?"

These thoughts don't usually announce themselves as optional commentary. They sneak in like facts. Like the truth. They masquerade as helpful little nudges toward improvement or responsibility, but really? They're just noise. And more often than not, they're lies.

One of the most freeing things I've ever learned is this: **Just because a thought pops into your head doesn't mean it's true.**

Thoughts are habits. And like any habit, they can become deeply ingrained over time—especially if they've been reinforced by experience, culture or well-meaning people who unintentionally passed down their own fears and insecurities.

But here's the good news: once you *notice* them, you can *change* them.

That's where your power lives. Not in shutting off every negative thought (impossible), but in recognizing that you don't have to automatically believe them. You can question them. Talk back. Reframe. You can ask, "Where did that come from?" or "Would I ever say that to someone I love?"

And maybe, just maybe, you'll start telling yourself a kinder, truer story.

FEELINGS AREN'T THE ENEMY

Let's clear something else up too: *feelings* are not the enemy. They're not evidence that something is wrong with you. They're not flaws to fix. They're not dramatic. And they're definitely not weaknesses.

In fact, they're built into your wiring.

From a cognitive behavioral therapy (CBT) perspective, there's a key distinction between *emotions* and *physiological feelings*. Emotions are the internal responses—things like sadness, anger, fear, joy. Feelings are the physical experiences those emotions create in your body. Like your chest tightening when you're anxious. Or your face flushing with embarrassment. Or that pit-in-your-stomach drop when something hits too hard.

Those sensations are your body's way of signaling something. They're not always convenient, but they are deeply human—and incredibly informative if we know how to listen.

Here's the reframe I wish we all got in school: **Emotions aren't flaws. They're flags.** They wave to get your attention. To say, "Hey, something's not sitting right here," or "This really matters to you," or "You're carrying too much, and your body is asking for a break."

We've been taught to suppress, ignore or override them. To "be strong" or "stay professional" or "not take it personally." But emotions don't go away when ignored. They just simmer underground—until they erupt, leak out sideways, or show up in our bodies as burnout, resentment, disconnection or even illness.

The goal here isn't to become emotionless. It's to become fluent. To learn the language of your feelings so you can respond with insight instead of shame. Because if you can pause and ask, *What is this emotion trying to tell me?* you've just taken a massive step toward alignment.

BEHAVIORS REVEAL THE STORY

If you ever want to know how you're *really* doing, look at your behaviors. Not the curated ones you put on display for others—the real ones. The patterns, the avoidances, the weird little habits that sneak in when no one's watching.

Because our behavior almost always tells the truth before we do.

Maybe you've stopped returning texts. Or you keep putting off that creative project you used to be excited about. Maybe you haven't read a book in months, even though reading has always been your positive escape. Maybe you're not doing anything obviously "bad," but you're also not doing much of anything at all—and that flatline is its own kind of alarm bell.

Here's the key insight: **inaction is a behavior, too.**

Avoiding. Delaying. Disengaging. Saying "yes" when you mean "no." Saying nothing when something needs to be said. These are behaviors. They are responses. And they are data.

They're clues that something is misaligned beneath the surface. And if we can get curious about what's *not happening*—what we're pulling away from, avoiding, ignoring—we might just uncover what's really going on. Sometimes we don't notice the shift until we realize, "I don't laugh as much anymore." Or, "I haven't felt excited in a long time." That's not laziness. That's a signal.

Behavior is the most visible part of the thoughts-feelings-behaviors triangle. And when it's off, it's often the first thing others notice—but the last thing we address. So take a look. Gently. Compassionately. What's missing? What's changed? And what might that be trying to tell you?

That's not failure. That's information. And it's exactly where the healing begins.

REFLECTION EXAMPLE: MY OWN DASHBOARD LIGHTS

For me, misalignment never arrives with flashing neon signs and dramatic proclamations.

It's quiet. Subtle. A slow fading out.

One of my first dashboard lights is skipping the rituals that make me feel like myself.

Reading in the bathtub—candles lit, soft music playing, a novel in hand—that's my happy place. That's where I exhale.

But when I'm overwhelmed or running on fumes, it's the first thing to go. Suddenly, even the idea of picking up a book feels like a chore. I tell myself I don't have time, or that I'll do it tomorrow, and then... I don't.

Another light blinks when I notice I'm not feeling joy—even in the moments where I should. Maybe I'm at a celebration or someone I love shares good news or something lovely happens in my day... and I feel nothing. Like I'm behind glass, watching life unfold but unable to reach it. That's dissociation. And for me, it's a warning bell with a really sharp tone.

Then comes the brittleness. The irritability. I snap more easily. I feel everything tightening in—my body, my calendar, my patience. I'm not laughing. I'm not engaging. I'm going through the motions.

These aren't just bad days. These are dashboard lights. My body and mind blinking red and saying, *"Hey... something's off."*

And here's the truth I've learned the hard way: those little warning signs? They don't fix themselves. They don't fade if you push through harder. They only get louder.

Tuning in to these patterns has been one of the most powerful forms of self-awareness I've ever cultivated. Because once I notice them, I can actually *do* something. Not fix everything overnight. But pause. Adjust. Ask for help. Say no. Carve space. Get back into alignment. But it starts with noticing.

TRY THIS: YOUR PERSONAL DASHBOARD CHECK

Think of this as your own internal check-engine light system. We're going to gently tune in and take stock—no judgment, just curiosity.

STEP 1: LIST YOUR "YOU" RITUALS

Write down 3–5 small things that make you feel most like yourself. These are the rituals, routines or moments that help you exhale. *(Examples: reading before bed, morning walks, journaling, calling a friend, playing music, cooking, playing with your pet, quiet time with coffee.)*

STEP 2: SCAN FOR MISSING PIECES

Now ask yourself:

- When was the last time I did each of these things?
- Have any fallen off lately?
- If yes—why? (Too busy, too tired, forgot they matter?)

STEP 3: BODY & MOOD CHECK

Take a moment to reflect:

- Is my body holding tension? Where?
- Do I feel easily irritated, snappy or flat?

- Am I going through the motions in any area of life?

STEP 4: LIGHT IT UP

For each ritual or area of well-being, rate your dashboard lights using this simple scale:

- Green = I'm good here.
- Yellow = I'm slipping a little.
- Red = Something needs my attention.

STEP 5: CHOOSE ONE SMALL RECONNECTION

What's one "yellow" or "red" light you can tend to this week? It doesn't have to be big. Maybe it's scheduling 30 minutes to read. Or texting a friend to set up coffee. Or just taking a deep breath and stretching your shoulders. Pick one thing —and make it happen.

Insight: These little reconnections are not luxuries. They're clues. Anchors. Your way back to alignment.

DEEP DIVE: THOUGHT SPIRALS IN ACTION

Not long ago, I got a text from my husband about our youngest daughter: "She's thinking of withdrawing from all her college classes." That was it. No context. No detail. Just that sentence—and my brain took off like a greyhound chasing a rabbit. Within seconds, I had built an entire disaster narrative.

- *She's going to ruin her GPA.*
- *She'll never recover from this.*
- *Why can't she just finish?*
- *This is a waste of tuition.*
- *Everyone's going to judge her. Or me.*
- *I must've done something wrong. I failed her.*

Before I'd even spoken to her, I was already halfway down a full-blown anxiety spiral. I wasn't responding to what was real—I was reacting to a story. A story I had written, directed, cast and produced entirely in my own head.

By the time I actually sat down to talk with her, I was in full meltdown mode. I wasn't calm, curious or supportive. I was anxious, frustrated and trying to fix something I didn't even understand yet.

I made the moment about me. My fear. My interpretation. My internal narrative. Not her struggle. Not her needs. Not the actual situation.

That's the thing about thought spirals—they feel true. They feel urgent. They feel like something we must *do* something about immediately. But they're not always grounded in fact.

Eventually, after a few deep breaths (and okay, a venting walk), I remembered: *I hadn't even asked her why.*

When I did, I learned she was overwhelmed—like deeply, sincerely struggling with a cocktail of burnout, perfectionism and stress. She wasn't giving up. She wasn't tanking her future. She was crying out for a break. For rest. For someone to *listen* before reacting.

And here's what I took from that moment:

- Anxiety often comes wearing the mask of control.
- When we spiral, we stop listening—to others *and* ourselves.
- Curiosity is what brings us back.

If I had paused to question those initial thoughts, "Is that true? Do I have enough information to know that?", I might have responded with compassion instead of panic. And honestly? I would've saved both of us a lot of unnecessary pain.

That's the gift of awareness. We don't have to believe every thought. We just have to notice them, name them and ask if they're actually serving us—or just running the show. Because when we interrupt the spiral, we make space for truth. And truth is what helps us realign.

REFLECTION EXERCISE:
TRACK THE TRIANGLE

Let's put this into practice because awareness without action is just trivia. Think back to a **recent emotionally charged moment.** It doesn't have to be a major life event; it could be something small that stuck with you—a tense meeting, an argument, a canceled plan, a snarky comment that rubbed you the wrong way. Pick one thing.

Remember the **Cognitive Behavioral Therapy triangle** we discussed earlier in the chapter? Grab a journal or notebook and walk through it with me as we process that emotionally charged moment:

1. WHAT THOUGHTS CAME UP?

What story did your brain immediately start telling? Was it something like:

- "They don't respect me."
- "I'm never going to get this right."
- "This always happens to me."

Write down the unfiltered version—no judgment. These are just automatic thoughts, not truths.

2. WHAT FEELINGS DID YOU EXPERIENCE— IN YOUR BODY?

Close your eyes and try to remember how your body responded.

- Did your chest tighten?
- Did your stomach drop?
- Did your pulse spike?
- Did your jaw clench?

Label the emotion if you can—anger, fear, shame, sadness—and describe how it physically showed up. (This is great data.)

3. WHAT BEHAVIORS FOLLOWED?

Now, what did you do (or *not* do) next?

- Did you withdraw?
- Pick a fight?
- Eat a sleeve of Oreos?
- Cancel plans?
- Stay up all night doom-scrolling?

Don't shame yourself—this is just observation. Behavior is a clue.

BONUS: REFRAME A THOUGHT.

Pick one of those automatic thoughts you listed. Ask yourself:

- Is this 100% true?
- Is there another way to look at this?
- What would I say if a friend told me this thought?

Then rewrite that thought in a gentler, truer way. For example:

- Original: *"I'm such a mess. I can't handle anything."*
- Reframe: *"I'm overwhelmed right now, but I'm doing the best I can—and that's enough."*

Now pause and imagine: If you had thought *that* instead, how might your behavior or emotion have shifted?

This is how we change the story. Not by force or perfection—but by noticing, naming and nudging ourselves into something more aligned.

One triangle at a time.

EMOTIONAL VOCABULARY:
THE FEELINGS WHEEL

When I was first learning how to name my emotions, I realized something both obvious and embarrassing: I didn't actually have the language. I could say I was "stressed" or "fine" or "mad," but beyond that? It was like trying to describe colors I'd never seen. And when you can't name what you're feeling, it's almost impossible to know what to do with it.

That's where the Feelings Wheel comes in—here's an example:

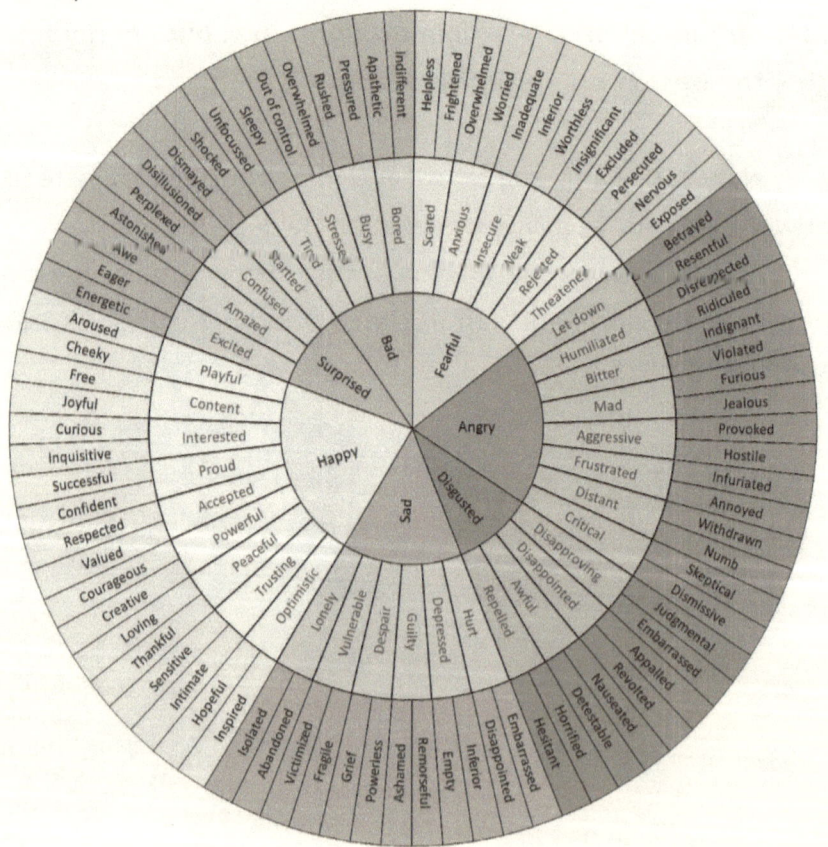

The Feelings Wheel is a deceptively simple tool that organizes emotions into six core categories—mad, sad, scared, joyful, powerful, and peaceful—and then expands into more nuanced descriptors like "insecure," "grateful," "anxious" or "hopeful." It's like a thesaurus for your inner world. And it's not just helpful—it's transformational.

Here's why this matters: the moment you can name an emotion, you take a layer of power back from it. The intensity often drops. It stops swirling in your body like an unnamed storm and instead becomes something specific you can work with. "I'm angry" is very different from "I feel disrespected." "I'm sad" is different from "I feel rejected." The more precise your vocabulary, the more clarity and compassion you can bring to yourself in real time.

When I'm overwhelmed or shut down, sometimes the most helpful thing I can do is literally pull up the Feelings Wheel and walk myself through it. What am I really feeling right now? Is it frustration or fear? Is it loneliness or exhaustion? I may start with a vague fog of "ugh," but with a little curiosity and the right words, I can almost always get to something clearer. And when I do, I can decide what I need, instead of flailing around in a mess of reaction.

This tool isn't about becoming hyper-analytical or assigning a label to every passing emotion. It's about building emotional fluency—so that you don't have to wait until your body is screaming at you to realize something's wrong. The Feelings Wheel helps you tune in sooner, with more accuracy and less judgment.

Take a moment to study the wheel. Notice which emotions feel familiar and which ones surprise you. Maybe even circle a few that you've felt this week. Just this small act of naming can be the beginning of something powerful.

CASE STUDY: THE VORTEX, REVISITED

Let's go back to my vortex for a minute—that season of life where everything felt like it was imploding at once. The job with the toxic boss. The house that should've come with its own horror soundtrack. The marriage slipping into a version of life I didn't recognize. The physical health scares. The commute. The pressure. The silence. I didn't have the tools then to name what was happening—I just knew it felt like drowning.

But now, with the lens of the cognitive triangle, I can see it more clearly. It wasn't one big, messy collapse. It was a system breakdown that started in my thoughts, flooded into my emotions and showed up in my behavior.

The thoughts?

"I can't trust myself."

"I make bad decisions."

"This is all my fault."

"Other people can handle life better than me."

The feelings?

Shame. Dread. Hopelessness.

Tight chest, stomach pain, that constant buzz of anxiety under my skin.

The behaviors?

Crying in the car. Picking fights with my partner. Isolating from friends. Fantasizing about disappearing—literally wishing I could vanish or be injured just enough to press pause on my life.

That's what happens when your internal dashboard is blinking red and you ignore every warning light. The system doesn't just whisper—it eventually screams. And in my case, I blew it all up. I walked away from everything, because I didn't see another option.

But here's the shift: now that I understand the triangle, I can catch myself sooner. I don't have to wait until I'm numb or spiraling or making impulsive escape plans. I can ask:

- What am I thinking right now, and is it actually true?
- What am I feeling and what's that feeling trying to tell me?
- Is how I'm acting reflective of who I want to be?

When I start skipping the things I love—when I'm too distracted to read, too brittle to engage, too overwhelmed to feel anything—I know it's time to check the system. The triangle gives me a map back to myself.

I didn't have this language back then. But I do now. And if you're in your own version of the vortex, I want you to know that learning to name the pieces can be the beginning of the way out. Not by force. Not by blowing everything up. But by listening—really listening—to what your thoughts, your feelings and your behavior are trying to say.

FINAL TAKEAWAYS:
EMOTIONS ARE ROAD SIGNS

If you take nothing else from this chapter, let it be this: **your emotions are not the enemy. They are road signs.** Not the final destination. Not your identity. Just signals—trying to get your attention, trying to help.

Feeling overwhelmed, stuck, numb, irritable, foggy or low-energy doesn't mean you're weak or broken. It means something is off. Something needs adjusting. Something inside you is waving a flag and saying, *"Hey... this doesn't feel right."*

We've been taught to ignore those flags. To rationalize them. To tough it out. To believe that if we just work harder, smile bigger or get more done, the feelings will eventually go away. But they don't go away. They amplify. They take root. And they start running the show from behind the scenes.

The goal isn't to eliminate hard feelings—that's not realistic and it's not even desirable. The goal is to **listen** to them. With curiosity. With grace. With just enough distance to say, *"This isn't all of me, but it is telling me something."*

That's what emotional fluency gives us: the power to **respond** instead of react. To pause. To pivot. To realign. When you're unsure, you can borrow Brené Brown's two genius questions:

1. Do I have enough data to freak out?
2. Will freaking out help?

Sometimes the answer might be yes. But more often, you'll realize that what you really need isn't a meltdown—it's a moment of *clarity*.

The better you get at speaking the language of your own emotions, the more clearly you'll see what truly matters to you—and the more equipped you'll be to build a life that honors that. ⊙⊶

CHAPTER NINE

Key: Scouts

What Have Other People Noticed

IT WAS ONE of our very first one-on-one meetings. Lynne, my new manager, had recently joined our group after rotating in from another HR division. I remember liking her energy right away—calm, clear, no-nonsense, but kind. She had that quiet confidence that didn't need to be announced or proven. We were sitting in one of the little glass-walled conference rooms on our floor, sipping coffee and running through the usual "get to know you" updates. And then, in the middle of the conversation, she looked at me and asked a question that completely threw me.

"Who are you proactively networking with outside of this group?"

I blinked. "Um, what?" I wasn't sure I heard her correctly. I thought I *was* doing great. I knew everyone on our floor. I was friendly. People liked me. I could name half the building on sight. But the way she asked the question made it clear that wasn't what she meant.

"You're a small fish in a very tiny pond," she said, without malice. "This division is only about ten percent of the overall company population. You need to start building relationships outside of this bubble if you want to grow."

Oof. I felt stung. Embarrassed. A little pride-bruised, if I'm being honest. I'd worked hard to become someone people respected and relied on and now here she was, telling me I was playing small. But there was something in the way she said it—direct but thoughtful—that made me pause. She wasn't dismissing my efforts. She was pointing to something larger. Something I couldn't see ... yet.

And she was right.

That one sentence—that moment—shifted something in me. Lynne wasn't criticizing me. She was *scouting* me. She saw potential I hadn't yet named for myself. She saw that I was capable of more than just being well-liked in my corner of the building. And instead of just saying "You have potential," she gave me a specific, uncomfortable-but-growth-filled action to take: go out and build relationships in new places.

Lynne was one of my first real **Scouts**—someone who not only recognized my natural gifts, but helped me use and refine them. She didn't just hand me a compliment. She handed me a direction.

This chapter is about exactly that. The people who notice us before we notice ourselves. The ones who quietly say, "Hey, have you ever thought about...?" or "You know, you're really good at this." And how often we dismiss those comments, brush them off or assume everyone must be able to do that thing—because it comes so easily to us, we can't see it as a talent.

Sometimes, we can't recognize our own reflection clearly until someone else holds up the mirror. Scouts do that for us. If we're open to it.

So let's talk about what other people have seen in you— and how that feedback might hold the keys to your next aligned step forward.

NOT ALL VALIDATION IS EXTERNAL PRAISE

Let's be real for a second—most of us are not walking around asking, "Hey, can you tell me what I'm great at?" In fact, for many of us, the idea of seeking feedback feels vulnerable in the worst way. Like it's an invitation for someone to discover we're actually a fraud. That we're *not* as good as they think. That we've been faking it all along and any minute now, some-one's going to say it out loud.

That tension—between shame and visibility—is power-ful. When we're already carrying a whisper of "not enough," the thought of being seen more fully, even positively, can feel terrifying. It's not always ego that keeps us from asking for help or clarity. It's fear. Fear that we'll be exposed. Fear that we're the only ones who don't have it figured out. Fear that if we ask someone to reflect what they see in us, they might shrug and say, "Honestly? Not much."

But here's what I've learned: strength spotting isn't about ego inflation. It's about *data collection*. And if you've been tracking with this journey so far, you'll remember that alignment is about noticing patterns—about treating your life like a series of hypothesis tests. Feedback from others is one more data point. Not a verdict. Not a life sentence. Just more information that can help you course-correct toward the life you actually want.

And that's the thing about feedback—it's not always wrapped in gold stars and glowing praise. Sometimes, it comes in the form of a manager like Lynne saying, "You're a small fish in a tiny pond," or a friend noticing something about your natural rhythm that you've never seen.

Feedback doesn't mean "you've arrived." It means *pay attention here.*

We're not meant to do this work alone in an echo chamber. The people around us—trusted, healthy, supportive people—can hold up a mirror to our gifts. Not to inflate us, but to remind us of what we might be overlooking. To name the things we've been too busy, too modest or too afraid to name for ourselves.

What if we stopped treating feedback like judgment and started treating it like guidance?

What might shift if we approached it not with dread, but with curiosity?

THE INFORMATIONAL INTERVIEW PROJECT

When Lynne gave me the assignment, I didn't fully realize what she was doing. She said, "Make a list of people outside your current division—people doing interesting work. Reach out. Set up one-on-one meetings. Just talk to them." Thirteen people. Over the next year. I didn't know it then, but she was helping me reroute my entire career.

It wasn't a casual suggestion—it was strategic. And it wasn't a punishment, either. It was a tailor-made growth opportunity. Because she saw me. She saw that I was naturally curious, that I could hold a conversation with anyone, that I asked thoughtful questions and genuinely wanted to learn. She knew I wasn't afraid to walk into a room or send a cold email. She matched the project to those strengths.

She helped me craft my list. I started setting up meetings. Every two or three weeks, I'd meet with someone new. And here's what's wild: every single person said yes. Some meetings lasted the scheduled 30 minutes; others went far longer. I came prepared with a list of questions—softball stuff, at first, to get them talking: Where are you from originally? What did you study in school? How did you end up here? What do you love about your role?

It was never awkward. Not once. These conversations flew by and I soaked it all up like a sponge. After each meeting, I sent a follow-up email—always personal, always appreciative. If they mentioned a hobby, I'd send an article related to it. If they voiced a challenge, I'd offer a helpful resource or connection. It was simple: I listened, followed up and stayed in touch.

Then something magical happened: *every single opportunity I was offered after that came directly from someone I'd met during this project*. Not some internal job board. Not applying cold. Not because I checked every box on a résumé. Because someone *knew me*—and remembered.

Looking back, I can see how strategic Lynne's approach was. She didn't assign this same task to everyone. She gave me something that fit my natural wiring and helped refine it into a professional superpower. She was, in every sense of the word, a *scout*.

REFLECTION PROMPT:

Think back—what opportunities or relationships have come into your life because someone noticed something about you? Was there a person who nudged you toward something that felt just out of reach? Who saw something in you before you could name it? Write that down. Capture it. That's data. That's you being seen.

THE ROLE OF SCOUTS

Scouts are the people who spot something in you—often long before you spot it yourself. But here's the part we often miss: scouts don't always arrive in dramatic fashion, waving flags and making speeches about your brilliance. Often, they're quiet observers. They drop a single sentence that lingers. They give you a nudge in a new direction. They say, "You're really good at that," in a tone so offhand you almost don't register it.

But you should.

Because those small comments are actually clues. They're data points. If enough people are saying the same thing—"You're such a great listener," "You have a way of bringing calm to chaos," "You always know how to explain complex ideas simply"—that's not coincidence.

That's a mirror.

The problem is, our gifts often feel invisible to us. Why? Because they come so naturally. We assume everyone else thinks that way, works that way, solves problems that way. We downplay. We deflect. We say, "Oh, that? That's nothing."

But if someone else sees it—and especially if more than one person sees it—then it's *something*.

Think about the people in your life who've noticed things you missed. A mentor who kept giving you the same kind of project. A friend who always calls you when they're going through something hard. A teacher who pulled you aside and said, "You've got something special." These are your scouts. And often, their insights are more reliable than your own self-assessments—because they're not muddied by your self-doubt.

You don't have to agree with everything someone sees in you. But you *do* owe it to yourself to pay attention. Because sometimes the quickest way to remember who you are is to see yourself through someone else's eyes.

THE DINNER COMPLIMENT

It started as an ordinary evening. I was moving through the kitchen, pulling random things from the fridge and pantry— half a bag of spinach, a bit of goat cheese, a lonely sweet potato, some chicken I'd defrosted that morning. Twenty minutes later, we had a full, balanced dinner on the table, and I didn't think twice about it.

But my husband looked at his plate, took a bite, and then looked at me and said, "You have a real knack for putting food together."

I blinked. "Um, what? You mean making dinner? That's just being a mom."

He shook his head. "No, it's more than that. You can see what we have, know what goes together, season it right, time it so everything's done at once. That's a talent."

I laughed at first. It felt silly to me. I wasn't doing any-thing special—I was just feeding my family. But he kept gently bringing it up. "Not everyone can do this," he'd say. "You make it look effortless."

I had to sit with that for a minute. And the truth? At first, I couldn't even see it. I really did assume everyone had this ability, like it was some kind of basic adulting skill. But as he started sharing stories of friends who got takeout for every meal or froze at the thought of cooking, I started to realize: oh. Not everyone does this. Not everyone *can* do this. It's not just "being a mom." It's something I'm good at. Something I enjoy. Something that, left unchecked, I would have completely dismissed.

Which is funny when you think about it—*I work in strengths for a living*. I spend my days helping other people identify and embrace their talents, and here I was, waving off my own.

That's how deeply conditioned we can be to downplay what comes naturally to us. And I think it's especially true for women. We're trained to brush off compliments, to deflect praise, to say, "Oh, it's nothing" rather than letting ourselves claim a win.

Here's my challenge to you: watch what you dismiss. Pay attention to where you deflect. If someone says you're great at something and your instinct is to brush it off, pause. Ask yourself: *What if they're right?*

You might be standing in the middle of your own genius and not even realize it.

TOM AND THE ENERGY OF CALM

From the moment I met Tom (my now husband), I knew there was something different about him. I don't typically go around talking about people's energy or vibes, but with him? It was unmistakable. Being around him felt like wrapping up in a warm blanket with someone whispering, *"It's going to be okay."* I've joked that he wears a cologne called "Everything Will Be Fine," and I still stand by that.

What's funny is that on paper, his resume screams intensity: Marine. Law enforcement. High-quota sales. The kind of jobs that conjure up grit, toughness and fast decision-making. And he does have those things—but what stands out most isn't the bravado. It's the calm. Tom has this incredible ability to enter a situation, no matter how charged or chaotic, and de-escalate it almost instantly. He brings people back to center, reminds them of their dignity and slows the emotional swirl until something solid emerges.

We've been out and about more times than I can count when an emergency unfolds—an accident, someone panicking, a tense exchange—and like clockwork, Tom steps in. It's not showy. It's not dramatic. But it's effective. It's like the universe quietly knows that when Tom shows up, things will settle.

According to Gallup's StrengthsFinder® assessment, Tom leads with the talent theme of **Connectedness®**. That theme is all about sensing the bigger picture—believing that we're all linked in some way, even if we can't quite explain how. It brings a deep sense of perspective and calm, a kind of soul-level steadiness that says, *we're going to figure this out to-gether*. People with Connectedness® are bridge builders. And that's exactly who Tom is. Whether he's solving a problem at work or talking down a tense room, he sees the humanity in everyone—and brings them together.

What I love about this is that it reframes something we often overlook. We tend to think of "strengths" as outward achievements—being fast, clever, commanding. But some-times a strength is quieter. Sometimes it's emotional presence. The ability to hold space, to stay grounded when others spin out. That isn't just a personality trait. It's a gift. A leadership superpower.

And if you've ever been on the receiving end of someone like Tom—someone whose very presence helps you breathe deeper—you know just how powerful that can be.

MINI REFLECTION PROMPT:
DOWNPLAYED COMPLIMENTS

Take a moment and think back—when was the last time someone gave you a compliment and you waved it off? Maybe someone said you were a great listener and you responded with, "Oh, I just nodded a lot." Maybe they praised your keen eye for color or your ability to stay calm under pressure and you brushed it off with, "It's nothing," or "Anyone could do that."

Here's the thing: deflection is often a neon sign that you're skipping right past one of your gifts. Not because it's not there—but because it feels so normal to you, you don't recognize it as special.

So pause. Think back to the compliment. What did they see in you? What skill or presence or talent were they pointing to? You don't have to fully agree with it yet. Just sit with it.

Let it be possible that someone else spotted something true and valuable in you.

This week, try this: when someone offers you a compliment, instead of batting it away, just say, *"Thank you."* That's it. And then maybe... write it down. That compliment could be a clue. A breadcrumb. A quiet truth you've been overlooking.

REFRAMING COMPLIMENTS AS CLUES

Here's something we rarely talk about: compliments are often treasure maps in disguise.

That casual "You're so organized," or "You always know what to say," or "I love how you styled this room" might seem like throwaway comments. But they're not. They're data points. Clues. Little red pins on the map of *you*.

The reason we tend to ignore them? Our true strengths usually feel easy to us. So easy, in fact, that we assume everyone else must find them easy, too. But that's not how strengths work.

Your effortless could be someone else's Everest.

When someone points something out—especially if you hear it more than once—pause before you brush it off. Could this be something that comes so naturally to you that you've stopped noticing it? Could it be a clue to what you're uniquely wired for?

One of the most powerful things we can do in the alignment process is to treat compliments not as ego boosts, but as information. They're not about arrogance. They're about accuracy. You don't have to turn every compliment into a career path—but if you start listening more closely, you might discover patterns. And those patterns are worth paying attention to.

REFLECTION EXERCISE: YOUR SCOUTS

It's time to pull out your metaphorical flashlight and look at some of the glowing signs others have held up for you—whether you noticed them at the time or not.

STEP 1: THINK BACK

Reflect on compliments, encouragement or positive feedback you've received—from childhood through now. These might've come from teachers, family, coworkers, managers, even strangers. No filter. Just jot it all down.

STEP 2: MAKE A LIST

Make a list of what people have told you you're good at. It could be anything:

- "You're such a great listener."
- "You're amazing at explaining things."
- "You just know how to throw a great party."
- "You always stay calm when things go sideways."
  Big or small, it all counts.

STEP 3: CIRCLE SURPRISES

Circle anything that surprised you—or that you dismissed in the moment. Maybe you shrugged it off, made a self-deprecating joke or thought, *Well, that's just something anyone would do.* Spoiler: it's probably not.

STEP 4: LOOK FOR PATTERNS.

Are there themes that emerge? Do these compliments fall into broader categories like:

- Creativity
- Compassion
- Problem-solving
- Communication
- Leadership
- Calm under pressure

- Organization
- Humor

If so, you're uncovering areas where you might naturally shine—places where alignment is waiting.

STEP 5 (OPTIONAL BUT POWERFUL): REACH OUT TO ONE TRUSTED PERSON AND ASK:

"What's something you think I'm naturally good at that I might not see in myself?"

You might be surprised—and deeply moved—by what they share. This isn't about fishing for praise. It's about pattern recognition. It's about seeing yourself more clearly, with the help of those who've been watching all along.

KEEPING A COMPLIMENT LOG

If you've ever doubted your gifts, or brushed off a kind word with, "Oh, that was nothing," I want you to try something that might feel a bit silly, but is surprisingly powerful: Start a compliment log.

That's right. Keep a running list—on your phone, in your journal, wherever you track your thoughts—of the positive things people say about you. It doesn't have to be formal or poetic. It can be as simple as:

- "Manager said I'm good at translating complicated ideas."
- "Friend told me I always know what to say when she's having a hard day."
- "Barista said I have a warm energy."

Think of this list as your **Scout File**—evidence gathered from the people who see you clearly, especially in the moments you don't see yourself. It's not about ego. It's about perspective. A breadcrumb trail of truths to revisit when imposter syndrome flares or self-doubt starts whispering louder than your intuition.

Over time, this file becomes more than a pick-me-up. It becomes **proof**—proof of who you really are and what comes naturally to you. And when you're ready to align your life with your true strengths, it will be one of your most valuable tools.

THE MAGIC OF ALIGNMENT:
WHEN TALENTS AND LIKES MEET

Here's where it all comes together: **alignment lives at the intersection of what you enjoy and what you're good at.**

That might sound simple, but it's where the real magic happens. Not the kind of magic that shows up with sparkles and a wand, but the deep, soul-level kind. The kind that feels like breathing easier. Like *you*—fully, confidently and without apology.

It's one thing to enjoy something. It's another to be good at it. But **when we align our likes with our talents, we make magic—and we make magic for others.** That's when work doesn't just feel productive—it feels meaningful. That's when your days start to reflect your values, your energy, your design.

And often? We don't get there alone.

That's why scouts matter. They don't just help us see what we're good at—they help us own it. They reflect back our potential before we're ready to believe in it ourselves. They give us the nudge, the perspective, the "have you ever thought about..." that shifts everything.

And when we listen—really listen—we begin to walk more boldly toward alignment. Toward the version of life that doesn't just *look* good on paper, but actually feels good in our bones.

Let yourself be seen. Let yourself be known. And let yourself believe that what you're good at—and what you love—deserve a place at the center of your life.

ACTIVITY: CREATE A "SCOUTS AND SIGNALS" BOARD

Sometimes we need to *see* things to believe them. That's where this exercise comes in. It's a visual way to capture the people who've seen your strengths—your **Scouts**—and the messages they've given you—your **Signals**.

Grab a journal page, whiteboard, poster or just a blank piece of paper. You can also create a digital version in something like Canva or Miro. Don't overthink the format—what matters is getting it out of your head and into view.

Here's how to do it:

STEP 1: DRAW A MIND MAP.
Write your name in the center. Around it, start adding the names of people who've said something kind, affirming or insightful about you. These are your Scouts—people who noticed something *true* about you, even if you couldn't see it yet.

STEP 2: CAPTURE THE SIGNALS.
Next to each person's name, jot down the specific praise or feedback they gave. Try to be as close to their original words as you can remember. Think about:
- Compliments from teachers, mentors, managers
- Comments from friends or family

- Moments someone called out your calm, your creativity, your clarity, your kindness

STEP 3: REFLECT ON EACH ONE.

Ask yourself:

- Did I believe it at the time?
- Did I deflect or dismiss it?
- Does it feel true to me now?
- Have I seen this theme show up in other areas of my life?

STEP 4: HIGHLIGHT PATTERNS.

Circle or star the comments that show up more than once. Is there a throughline? Are you always the one who brings the calm? Solves the puzzle? Organizes the chaos? Sparks the laughter?

This is your *Scouts and Signals* board—a collection of truth-tellers who saw your gifts, even when you couldn't. Keep it somewhere you'll revisit. Add to it over time.

Because when doubt creeps in—and it will—you'll have a visual reminder:

- You've been seen.
- You've been affirmed.
- And your gifts are *real*.

YOU HAVE GIFTS THE WORLD NEEDS

If there's one thing I hope you walk away with from this chapter, it's this: *you have gifts*. Real, valuable, deeply needed gifts. Even if you can't see them clearly yet. Even if they feel too small or too ordinary. Even if you've brushed them off, minimized them or hidden them under layers of self-doubt or survival.

If even one person has noticed something special in you—it matters. That compliment you shrugged off? That moment someone asked for your help in a way that felt oddly specific? That spark of ease you feel when doing something that lights you up? Those are all clues. Invitations to keep exploring.

You don't have to be 100% confident in your strengths right now. You don't have to have a polished, perfect picture of what you're meant to do or who you're becoming. You can *borrow someone else's belief* for a little while. That's what scouts are for.

Just keep showing up. Keep noticing. Keep listening.

And most of all, keep building a relationship with your gifts—one reflection, one small yes, one brave step at a time.

The world doesn't need a shinier, more impressive version of you. It needs *the real you*—the one you're already becoming. ⚷

CHAPTER TEN

Key: Engagement

When we hear the word *engagement*, we often think of annual surveys, HR presentations or leadership training seminars. Thanks to Gallup's research, terms like *engaged*, *not engaged* and *actively disengaged* have become part of the corporate vocabulary. They're useful, sure—but this chapter isn't about workplace metrics.

It's about *you*.

Because engagement doesn't just matter to your boss—it matters to your body. It's not just about how you show up for your job. It's about how you show up for your *life*.

So let's reframe the question.

Not: "Are you engaged at work?"

But: **"What does being engaged feel like—for you?"**

Not just when you're sitting in a meeting or checking off to-dos. But in your real life. In your mind, your body, your energy. When do you feel fully present? Curious? Focused? When do you feel resistant, checked out or like you're moving through mud?

That question is the heartbeat of this chapter. And to really understand it, I want to start by sharing a story.

WHEN WORK AND VALUES COLLIDE

For years, I had a steady, long-standing client—a state agency where I was brought in regularly to lead professional development and strengths-based workshops. I liked the work. I liked the people. I especially liked my point of contact, who was receptive, kind and collaborative. It felt aligned.

Then leadership changed.

The new director had a completely different energy. Brash. Condescending. And—most alarming to me—he wanted to use StrengthsFinder® results to single out people on his team he didn't like. To weaponize them.

The work no longer felt empowering. It felt complicit.

At first, I brushed it off. I told myself it was temporary. I told myself I could protect the team from the worst of it. I told myself I was imagining things.

But my body knew better.

- My chest clenched every time an email came through from him.
- My stomach knotted at the idea of another meeting.
- I started complaining more. Snapping more.

- I could feel the resentment creeping in—and worse, the *numbness*.

Eventually, I realized this wasn't just a bad client fit. It was a values breach. I couldn't stand behind the work the way it was being handled. So I did something hard: I gave notice, wrapped up the project and stepped away.

Immediately, I felt lighter. My shoulders relaxed. My stomach unclenched. My energy came back online. That moment taught me something I return to again and again:

Your body knows. Before your mind can articulate the misalignment, your body already feels it. Before the thought comes, the tension speaks.

We spend so much time trying to *think* our way into or out of situations. But often, our *energy* is the more honest communicator. If you want to understand your state of engagement, don't just analyze your output. Listen to your body. Trace your energy.

This chapter is going to help you do exactly that. Ready to begin?

INTRODUCING THE GALLUP ENGAGEMENT MODEL

Over the last two decades, Gallup's global research on engagement has shaped how organizations think about performance, retention and well-being. Their framework breaks employee engagement down into three clear categories, each defined by specific attitudes and behaviors.

Let's walk through those categories:

1. ENGAGED

- These are the people who are involved, enthusiastic and emotionally invested in what they're doing.
- They show up consistently—with energy, focus and a genuine desire to contribute.
- They don't just do what's required; they offer solutions, collaborate well and find meaning in their work.
- Gallup data shows that engaged individuals are more productive, have fewer quality issues, take fewer sick days and are generally more satisfied and resilient.

2. NOT ENGAGED

- This category represents the "meh" zone.
- These individuals are present but not connected. They're doing the minimum, often just going through the motions.
- They're not actively sabotaging the work—but they're not bringing enthusiasm or
- creativity to it either.
- Gallup often describes this group as "checked out"— physically there but emotionally distant.

3. ACTIVELY DISENGAGED

- This is where things get tricky—and sometimes toxic.
- Actively disengaged people aren't just unmotivated—they're resentful, cynical and may be working against the goals of the team or organization.
- They might gossip, miss deadlines, criticize others or subtly undermine the work of teammates.
- Gallup found that this group creates a disproportionately negative ripple effect, dragging down morale, productivity and workplace culture.

WHAT THE RESEARCH TELLS US

Gallup's findings are consistent and compelling:

- Higher levels of engagement correlate with better performance outcomes across every industry.
- Engaged employees report fewer health issues, lower stress levels and higher job satisfaction.
- Companies with high employee engagement see increased retention, loyalty, creativity and customer satisfaction.

But here's the critical shift this chapter makes: *This isn't just about your workplace. This is about your life.*

You don't need a boss or a paycheck to apply these categories. Engagement is a state of being, not a job title. You can be:

- Engaged in your parenting
- Not engaged in your friendships
- Actively disengaged from your own creative pursuits

In other words—this is personal.

You've probably *felt* all three states. You just may not have had the language to describe them. That's what we're going to unpack next. You'll learn to name your state of engagement, notice when it shifts and figure out what to do about it—so you can spend more of your time in alignment with who you actually are.

REFLECTION EXERCISE: WHAT DO THESE STATES LOOK LIKE FOR YOU?

We're going to take Gallup's three engagement categories (Engaged, Not Engaged and Actively Disengaged) and apply them to your real life.

This is not about job performance or office politics. It's about noticing your own energy, presence and alignment across the moments of your day—at work, at home and everywhere in between. Take your time with each category. Be honest. No one else is reading this but you.

ENGAGED

This is your *"I'm all in"* mode. You're present. Energized. Maybe even excited. You're using your natural talents and feeling like your true self.

- What am I doing when I feel this way?
  (Think: types of tasks, activities, environments.)
- Who am I with?
  (Is there a person or group that draws this out in you?)
- What time of day or day of week is it?
  (Do you have natural rhythms that support engagement?)
- How would someone else know I'm in this state?
  (What would they see, hear or notice?)
- What percentage of time do I spend here, on average?
  (Be honest—even 10% is a place to build from.)

NOT ENGAGED

This is your *autopilot* mode. You're physically present but emotionally checked out. You're doing what's required, but not much more.

- What am I doing when I feel this way?
  (Think: routine tasks, interactions, obligations.)
- Who am I with?
  (Anyone you tend to feel flat or neutral around?)
- What time of day or day of week is it?
  (Is there a pattern or slump?)
- How would someone else know I'm in this state?
  (Are you quieter? Distracted? Less responsive?)
- What percentage of time do I spend here, on average?

ACTIVELY DISENGAGED

This is your *"I don't want to be here"* mode. You might feel irritable, drained, resistant or even resentful. You're not just neutral—you're off.

- What am I doing when I feel this way?
  (Think: specific responsibilities, environments, conversations.)
- Who am I with?
  (Be honest—some people leave us depleted.)
- What time of day or day of week is it?
  (When do you notice your lowest energy or resistance?)
- How would someone else know I'm in this state?
  (What does it look like or sound like externally?)
- What percentage of time do I spend here, on average?
  (Even a small percentage is important to notice.)

OPTIONAL BONUS:

After you've reflected, ask yourself:

- What would help me increase time in the Engaged zone?
- What can I shift or reframe about my Not Engaged moments?
- What boundaries or changes would reduce my Actively Disengaged time?

You don't need to overhaul everything at once. Noticing is the first powerful step. Ready to keep going? Let's explore how your body can guide you.

THE PERSONAL ENGAGEMENT AUDIT
(GREEN / YELLOW / RED)

I've developed a system I use at least twice a year to take stock of how I'm spending my time and energy. It's simple, color-coded and surprisingly clarifying. I call it my **Personal Engagement Audit**, and here's how it works:

- **Green** = *Aligned, fulfilling, energizing.* These are the projects, people or parts of life that feel like they were made for me. I'm excited to show up. I feel proud of the work I'm doing. I'd happily do it again.

Yellow = *Neutral, "meh," tolerable*. These aren't disasters. They're just... OK. I can get through them, but they don't spark anything. Something's off—whether it's the timing, the dynamic or the setup. If something changed, it *could* be great—but as is, it's lukewarm.

- **Red** = *Draining, misaligned, should be avoided*. These are the energy vampires. The things that make your stomach knot or your chest tighten. The people or projects that leave you snippy, procrastinating or second-guessing yourself. When I'm in a red-zone situation, even if I deliver just fine externally, I know internally it's costing me something.

Every six months or so, I sit down with a spreadsheet of recent work—clients, projects, partnerships—and I **color-code** each line item.

- **Green**: I loved this. I felt proud of what I contributed, I liked the client I worked with and the work I did, I'd do it again in a heartbeat.

- **Yellow:** This was fine, but something dulled the spark. I note what that something was: maybe the prep was exhausting, the turnaround too tight or the communication unclear.

- **Red:** Even if the client loved it, I didn't. Maybe I felt drained every time their name popped up in my inbox.

Maybe I delivered with professionalism, but inside I was gritting my teeth. That's not sustainable. And if I'm honest, I often knew it was red **before** I officially admitted it to myself.

WHY THIS WORKS:

It takes the emotional swirl out of decision-making. I don't have to rely on memory or mood. I have data: color-coded reminders of how I actually felt during and after each engagement.

It also helps me decide what to pursue more of, what to shift and what to let go of—even if the money, prestige or ego stroke says "yes."

This system isn't just for work. You can do it for:

- Weekly commitments
- Social events
- Household responsibilities
- Volunteering
- Family routines
- Personal habits

If you leave a dinner party and feel lit up? That's green.

If you're just clocking time at book club but not really enjoying it? That's yellow.

If you dread answering a group text or always feel worse after a certain interaction? That's red.

It's a simple but powerful tool to help you live more in alignment—and recognize when your energy is trying to send you a message.

REFLECTION ACTIVITY:
MAP YOUR WEEK IN COLORS

Let's get practical. Now that you understand the green/yellow/red framework, it's time to apply it to your actual life.

INSTRUCTIONS:
Look at your **typical week**—not your dream week or your worst-case week, just your average one. For each major part of your day, assign a color based on how that activity **feels** to you.
Be honest. This is just for you.

COLOR KEY:
- **Green** = Aligned, energizing, fulfilling. You leave this activity feeling lit up or grounded.
- **Yellow** = Neutral, meh, tolerable. It's not awful but something feels off or missing.
- **Red** = Draining, misaligned, tension-filled. This one takes more than it gives.

1. MORNING ROUTINE
- What color would you assign your mornings?
- Do you wake up energized or already behind?
- Is your routine something you enjoy—or something you just survive?

2. JOB RESPONSIBILITIES
- Break this down if needed (meetings, emails, deep work, commuting).
- What parts of your work feel green? Yellow? Red?
- Are you spending most of your energy where it matters?

3. TIME WITH FAMILY OR FRIENDS
- Think about who you spend time with and how you feel during and after.
- Does this time leave you feeling seen and supported—or drained and invisible?

4. ERRANDS & CHORES
- Nobody loves cleaning the fridge. But some people find satisfaction in a tidy kitchen or a crossed-off to-do list.
- Is there any part of your upkeep that feels green? Or are these tasks edging toward red?

5. CREATIVE WORK OR HOBBIES

- Are you carving out space for things that fill your tank?
- Do you feel inspired and engaged—or is your creative time getting squeezed out by everything else?

Now, Look for Patterns:

- **What activities are consistently green?**
  Can you expand them, prioritize them or build more of your schedule around them?
- **What tasks feel yellow or red—and why?**
  Are they misaligned with your values? Is it the task itself or the way it's currently set up?
- **Is there anything yellow that's trending red?**
  Pay attention here. A yellow that starts feeling like a "meh" can quickly become a "nope" if ignored too long.

This isn't about overhauling your entire life in one go. It's about **noticing**. Because when you notice... you get to choose. And choice is where alignment begins.

LISTENING TO THE BODY

Let's go back to that state agency client I mentioned earlier—not to rehash the story, but to spotlight something important that was happening underneath the surface: **my body knew first.**

Before I had fully admitted the misalignment in my mind, my body had already raised its hand. My chest tightened every time I saw an email from their new leadership. My stomach twisted. My shoulders crept up to my ears. And I was crankier than usual—short with people I loved, more sensitive to everyday frustrations. I chalked it up to being busy. To stress. To a bad week. But it wasn't a moment. It was a message.

And here's the thing: I do this work for a living. I teach people how to tune into what they're feeling and make values-aligned decisions. And still, it took me a while to catch up to what my body was already screaming.

That's the power of **embodied awareness**. Long before you rationalize a decision, long before your brain starts crafting a narrative about whether something is "worth it" or "normal," your nervous system is keeping score. We'll go into more detail on body responses in an upcoming chapter.

When we're out of alignment—when we're saying yes to things that violate our values, or tolerating environments that slowly eat away at our peace—our body doesn't wait. It whispers... then nudges... then, if we ignore it long enough, it shouts.

Pay attention to those early cues:

- The tension in your jaw
- The sigh that comes every time you open your laptop
- The procrastination that doesn't feel lazy—it feels protective

You don't need to wait until burnout or breakdown to take action. Start with noticing.

Because the body rarely lies.

LISA'S PRESTIGE GIG TURNED SOUL-SUCK

Let me tell you about my friend Lisa—one of the most dynamic, joyful, magnetic professionals I know. Truly, if the word "powerhouse" had a picture next to it in the dictionary, it would be Lisa in a bold lipstick, blazer, with a great microphone, lighting up a virtual room or crushing it on stage. She radiates positive energy and has an incredible gift for connecting with people. It's one of the reasons she landed what seemed like a dream gig with a prestigious client.

The opportunity came with all the bells and whistles—recognizable brand name, steady income, credibility with a capital "C." It was the kind of client that made people pause mid introduction and nod with impressed approval. For someone who thrives on building connection and trust, it felt like a massive win.

At first, everything went great. Lisa dove into the work with her usual brilliance. The people were kind. The students she trained were engaged. She was making an impact. But over time, the invisible costs started stacking up.

There were hours and hours of administrative tasks she hadn't expected—outside the scope of the contract, unpaid and exhausting. The content was pre-scripted down to the word, which left little room for her signature magic. She was suddenly spending ten extra hours a week doing compliance training, jumping through tech hoops and managing a finicky platform—not for one session, but again and again, for every new cohort they handed her.

It didn't happen overnight, but little by little, something shifted. The work started to drain her. The energy she used to bring so naturally turned into something she had to manufacture. She began to feel resentful. Her signature pep—the part of her that felt light and engaged—was fading.

The kicker? It wasn't that the job was terrible. In fact, from the outside, everything still looked amazing. The client was still lovely. The mission was still aligned. But the *energy* told a different story. And Lisa, being the self-aware person she is, finally paid attention to what her body and spirit were saying.

She made the call to step away—graciously, professionally, respectfully. And the moment she did? She felt free. Like her energy came surging back. Her time opened up. Her ideas flowed. She described it as "lightness," like her whole body exhaled for the first time in months.

Lisa's story is such a powerful reminder: **just because something looks good on paper doesn't mean it's a green light for your soul.**

Sometimes the opportunities that once lit us up start pulling us under. And when they do, it's not failure to walk away. It's wisdom.

If your body is whispering (or screaming), if your calendar is full but your spirit feels flat—pay attention. Your energy never lies.

REFLECTION EXERCISE: TRACE YOUR ENGAGEMENT ENERGY

Let's pause here and do a little internal audit—not with your brain, but with your **body**.

Think of this as an energy trace. No spreadsheets or scorecards, just honest noticing.

Ask yourself:

- Where in your life do you feel light, energized and "peppy"? (Think about your work, relationships, creative projects, errands—anything. What gives you that electric hum, where time flies and you feel most like *you*?)

- Where do you feel constricted, drained or resentful? (Notice the areas that come with a sigh. The meetings that make you clench your jaw. The social obligations that leave you emotionally hungover. The tasks that always get pushed to tomorrow.)

- What does your body say about your calendar? (Sit with your upcoming week. What makes your shoulders drop with relief? What tightens your chest or gives you that low-simmer dread? These physical responses are data— pay attention.)

- What are you tolerating because it "looks good on paper"? (Maybe it's a client with name recognition, a role with a fancy title or a friendship that everyone else thinks is #goals. But if you're secretly fantasizing about canceling, quitting or ghosting... something's off.)

Take five minutes. Jot down what comes up without judgment. No need to fix anything yet—just get curious.

Because the first step to shifting your energy is seeing where it's leaking.

DISENGAGEMENT IS NOT A MORAL FAILING

Let's get something straight: feeling disengaged doesn't mean you're lazy. Or selfish. Or broken. It means you're human.

We all move through **green**, **yellow** and **red** zones— sometimes in a single day. Sometimes within the same hour. The goal isn't to live your entire life in "green." That's not realistic. Or necessary.

But what *is* necessary?

- Awareness.
- Honest self-assessment.
- The willingness to notice when something isn't working.

Being in a "not engaged" or "actively disengaged" space isn't a personal failure—it's a **flag**. A signal that something needs attention, whether it's your workload, your environment, your values or your energy reserves.

And if you've been hanging out in yellow or red longer than you'd like to admit, please hear this: *You don't have to stay there*. But first, you have to name it. That's where change begins—not from guilt, but from clarity.

BUILD YOUR ENGAGEMENT FILTER

Now that you've started mapping your energy zones, it's time to get even more intentional. Think of this as building your **Engagement Filter**—a personalized checklist to help you recognize the green lights in your life *before* you commit time, energy or emotion.

These aren't universal answers. This is about *you*. So grab a notebook or open your notes app and answer these prompts honestly, even if the answers surprise you.

1. WHAT KIND OF PEOPLE ENERGIZE ME?

Think about people who make you feel more like yourself when you're around them. Are they curious? Kind? Visionary? Grounded? Are they collaborators or deep thinkers?

Who leaves you lit up after a conversation—and who leaves you drained?

2. WHAT KIND OF WORK OR TASKS MAKE ME FEEL PURPOSEFUL?

What do you love to create, organize, fix, explore, teach or lead?

When do you lose track of time in a good way?

What kind of work makes you proud *while* you're doing it—not just once it's done?

3. WHAT TIME OF DAY AM I MOST ALIGNED?

Everyone has natural rhythms. Maybe you come alive mid-morning, get an energy boost at night or think best on walks.

When are you most clear-headed, motivated or creative?

4. WHAT WARNING SIGNS SIGNAL YELLOW OR RED?

These are your dashboard lights. Start noticing patterns.

- Tight chest?
- Procrastination?
- Constant sighing or snippy replies?
- Endless dread or fantasizing about canceling everything?

These signals are worth tracking. They're not overreactions. They're information.

When you start filtering decisions, commitments and relationships through this lens, life gets clearer. You start choosing green on purpose—and noticing red before it hijacks your peace.

FINAL TAKEAWAY: ENERGY IS DATA

Your state of being isn't just a footnote in your story—it *is* the story.

Every sigh, every surge of excitement, every low-grade dread you feel walking into a room or opening your laptop? It's information. Your body is whispering (or sometimes shouting) truths your brain hasn't caught up to yet.

You don't have to justify misalignment to anyone. You don't have to wait until things are falling apart or making you sick. You don't have to *earn* your way out of something that's no longer right for you. You just have to notice. That's it. Noticing is the beginning of alignment. Noticing is how you start to shift. Noticing is how you come home to yourself.

You weren't meant to power through life numb, depleted or disconnected. You were meant to live with intention—choosing the things, people and work that make you feel most alive.

So pay attention to the signals. Trust what they're trying to tell you. Because your energy is never random.

It's a compass.

It's pointing somewhere.

And you get to decide whether to follow it. ⚷

CHAPTER ELEVEN

Key: Your Best Work Day

WHENEVER I START working with a new client, I always ask the same question: *"What do you want?"* And almost every single time, the answer comes back in some version of: *"I just want to be happy."*

It sounds reasonable, right? Who doesn't want to be happy? But I've learned to pause here. Because while that answer feels like a full sentence, it's actually more like a placeholder. A shorthand way of saying, *"I'm not okay with where I am, but I haven't quite figured out where I want to go."*

And that's where we get stuck.

Imagine this: You're in Dallas. You walk into a travel agency (just go with me here—it's 1996) and say, *"Hi, I'd like a ticket to... not Dallas."*

The agent blinks. "Okay... where exactly do you want to go?"

You shrug. "I don't know. Just somewhere else. Not here."

Sounds ridiculous, right? But this is exactly how most of us approach our dissatisfaction. We don't like where we are but we haven't defined what we're moving toward. And when we don't know where we're going, we spin in circles. We feel frustrated that things aren't improving but we're not giving ourselves a destination—just the desperate hope of *"not here."*

The problem is that "not here" isn't a strategy. It's a signal.

And that's what this chapter is about.

We're not going to talk about happiness as a vague emotional ideal. We're going to talk about what actually works— for you. We're going to get specific. Tangible. Practical.

Because the fastest way to move toward alignment is to start noticing what's already working. Not in theory, not in big life vision statements but in real life. Real moments. The stuff that lights you up on an ordinary Tuesday.

Let's find your version of "happy"—not as an abstract concept but as a lived, repeatable experience you can build more of. Starting with your best day at work.

REFRAMING THE QUESTION:
FROM ESCAPE TO INTENTION

It's completely normal to want out of something that's making you feel stuck, drained or misaligned. We've all had moments— maybe weeks, maybe years—of thinking, *"Anywhere but here."* That's human.

But here's the tricky part: the urgency to escape can sometimes overshadow the clarity of direction. We spend all our energy running away from the discomfort without ever stopping to ask—*Where exactly am I trying to go?*

Escape is a reaction. Intention is a decision.

And if we want to build lives that actually fit—lives that feel like ours—we have to start trading in vague dissatisfaction for specific insight. Alignment doesn't just happen because we wish hard enough. It happens because we notice patterns. We pay attention. We get curious about what actually works, not just what we want to avoid.

One of the most powerful tools I've found for doing that? Studying your own best day at work.

Not the fantasy version, not the Pinterest-perfect dream job. I'm talking about a real, lived moment from your actual life where something clicked. Where you felt useful, energized, maybe even proud. Where your time felt well spent. Where something about that day made you think, *"Yes. More of this, please."*

That moment holds more data than a dozen personality quizzes. Because it's not hypothetical—it's you, in motion, doing something that worked. Something that fit.

So let's shift the question.

Not just *"How do I get out?"*

But instead *"What's already working—and how can I build more of that?"*

THE BMW DEALERSHIP FIELD TRIP

I was handed an assignment from corporate: deliver an 8-hour customer service training to my team. Eight.Hours. Of.PowerPoint.

I opened the materials and instantly felt my soul deflate. Eight hours of slides reminding us that treating customers well was a good idea—as if that were a groundbreaking concept. It felt like being asked to throw a birthday party with a list of required talking points and a ban on cake.

I couldn't do it.

Something in me just snapped. I could not stand in front of my team, click through that deck, and pretend it was the best way to inspire anyone to care more about the customer experience.

So I scrapped the slides and planned a field trip instead.

I rented a bus. I ordered sack lunches. And I told the team we were leaving the office for the day to experience exceptional customer service in action.

Our destination? A local BMW dealership. Not because it was fancy, but because it had a story.

This dealership had once been a customer service nightmare—bottom 5 among dealerships in the entire country. Then new leadership came in and everything changed. But not through some dramatic overhaul. They kept the same staff, the same bones of the place. What they changed was the mindset.

They asked every employee to treat each customer like they were their favorite grandmother. You know the one—the soft, cookie-baking, arms-wide-open kind of grandmother.

"What would make her feel cared for?" became the new operating question.

One of the departments named her Betsy. Would you make Grandma Betsy wait two hours for her car next to a pile of smelly tires? Would you low ball her trade-in? Would you make her sit in a hot garage bay with a rude technician and a deafening air gun?

No. You'd move mountains to make her feel valued. She's your favorite.

That shift changed everything. They added thoughtful touches. They air-conditioned the service bays. They let the techs wear shorts (a huge deal in hot and humid Texas). They washed every serviced car before returning it. They sent hand-signed birthday cards.

And it worked. Customers noticed. Staff morale improved. Turnover dropped. They skyrocketed from almost dead-last in satisfaction to one of the top-performing dealerships in the country.

As I watched my team hear this story, something beautiful happened. Their faces lit up. They asked questions. They leaned in. And then, best of all, they started dreaming up how to apply those same principles to our own customer experience. The conversations that followed weren't forced—they were organic, inspired, electric.

It was one of my best days at work.

Not because I love arranging transportation or sourcing sack lunches (I do not). But because I had the freedom to make something better. To bring a concept to life in a way that actually landed. That meant something.

Here's what worked for me:

- **Creative autonomy** – I got to design the experience from scratch.
- **Real-world learning** – No theory. Just seeing excellence in action.
- **Positive feedback loop** – The team was engaged, inspired and energized.
- **Shared experience and connection** – We bonded over something meaningful.
- **Values-based impact** – It wasn't just training. It was transformation.

That day taught me something critical: When the work aligns with how I'm wired—curious, creative, connection-oriented—I come alive. Even if some of the logistics are annoying, the overall experience fuels me.

And that's what we're looking for—not perfect days, but patterns. Clues. What parts of your past work made you feel most alive?

Let's find more of that.

REFLECTION EXERCISE:
RECONSTRUCT YOUR BEST WORK DAY

Think back to a time when you felt energized, fulfilled and like you were exactly where you were supposed to be. This could have been a paid job, a school project, volunteer work or even a time you were organizing something for your family or community.

Let's break it down so you can mine it for the gold:

1. **What was happening?** Describe the event, project or day as clearly as you can. Was it a presentation? A team retreat? A solo creative day? A high-stakes challenge you crushed?

2. **Who else was involved?** Were you collaborating with others or flying solo? Were you leading, supporting, teaching, brainstorming, managing, creating?

3. **What exactly did you enjoy?** Don't stop at "It was fun." What *specifically* made it enjoyable? Was it the creative freedom? The problem-solving? The interaction with others? The ability to go deep and focus? The fun t-shirt you designed?

4. **What role were you playing?** Were you the idea generator? The organizer? The connector? The closer? Think about the metaphorical hat you were wearing and how it fit.

5. **How did it make you feel—physically and emotionally?**
   Light? Energized? Peppy? Grounded? Like time flew by? Like you were in flow? Were you smiling? Did your body feel relaxed or buzzy with energy?

6. **Was it a one-time thing or a recurring experience?**
   Was this a magical one-off... or a regular part of your life that's since faded? (And if so, do you miss it?)

7. **What part of it would you love to do again?** Name the parts that lit you up. Even if it's just a sliver of the day— those are your *green lights*.

8. **What part would you skip?** Even on great days, there are pieces that drain us. Be honest about the bits you could happily hand off.

Now go ahead and write it down. Be as specific as possible. The more details, the better. You're creating a blueprint for what alignment looks and feels like *in real life*—so you can intentionally build more of it.

Because the best days aren't always accidents. Sometimes, they're data.

ZOOMING IN: IT'S THE ELEMENTS,
NOT THE WHOLE

Here's where a lot of us get tripped up: we assume that in order for something to "count" as a best day, *every single part* of it has to be perfect.

But real life? It's rarely that tidy.

Alignment doesn't mean every detail was dreamy. It means that *enough of the right pieces* were present—the ones that light you up, connect to your values and bring you alive. Having enough of the right pieces give us the energy to navigate and persist through the not-so great stuff.

Take that BMW field trip day. Was I thrilled about organizing sack lunches, wrangling buses or confirming schedules with a dozen people? No. Not even a little. Logistics don't live on my "best of" list. But those details weren't the *point*. They were the scaffolding for what actually mattered.

What *did* matter?

- The creative autonomy to scrap the dull, ineffective training plan and design something better.
- The sense of purpose in spotlighting real-world excellence.
- The shared learning, laughter and aha moments as people made connections back to our own work.
- The ripple effect it had afterward—people still talking about it, still applying the insights. That's the magic. That's what I would replicate again and again.

So don't write off an experience just because part of it was hard or tedious. Instead, **zoom in** and ask:

- What *exactly* made this meaningful?
- What *element* would I love to do more of?
- What can I leave behind next time?

You're not chasing perfect. You're chasing alignment. And that lives in the details.

REFLECTION PROMPT: WHAT WERE THE BUILDING BLOCKS?

Let's get even more granular.

Your best days—those moments when you felt present, lit up and like the truest version of yourself—aren't accidents. They're made up of specific ingredients. And once you can name those building blocks, you can start intentionally adding more of them into your life.

Take a few minutes to sit with the prompts below. Answer honestly, without overthinking.

There are no "right" responses—just real ones.

I feel most alive when I'm

_____.

I'm proud of myself when I

_____.

I lose track of time when I'm

_____.

People thank me most often for

_____.

I would choose to do more of _____

_____ **if no one was watching**

or judging.

What do you notice?

Which words or themes show up more than once?

Where are the clues pointing?

This is how we stop chasing vague "happiness" and start designing alignment—one building block at a time.

MICRO-MOMENTS OF MAGIC

Not every "best day" is going to involve a field trip, a bold decision or a sweeping breakthrough. In fact, some of the most revealing indicators of alignment are tucked quietly into your regular, unremarkable days.

Maybe it's the satisfying click of finishing a project. Or the buzz of solving a tricky problem no one else wanted to tackle.

Maybe it's a friend texting, "Thank you, that really helped." Or a coworker saying, "You always make this easier."

Maybe it's just that one meeting where someone made you laugh and for a moment, your shoulders dropped and your breath came easier.

These small sparks? They matter. They're data. They're direction. They're pieces of your best day, showing up in real time.

We often overlook these micro-moments because they don't feel "big enough." But alignment doesn't always arrive with a banner and confetti. Sometimes it whispers. You just have to learn to hear it.

REFLECTION EXERCISE: THE PATTERN SPOTTER GRID

Let's turn your aligned moments into something you can actually use.

We're going to zoom out and start noticing *patterns*. Because alignment isn't usually about one big event—it's about recurring elements that energize and inspire you. The more we can identify those elements, the more we can intentionally build them into our life and work.

INSTRUCTIONS:

1. Think back on moments—big or small—where you felt lit up, purposeful, proud, engaged or at peace.
2. Use the table below to capture what made those moments work for you.
3. Don't overthink it. This is about your experience, not what "should" matter.
4. Try to fill in at least one row for each category: *Environment*, *Task*, *Role* and *Interaction*.

Element	Description	Why It Energized Me	How to Get More of It
Environment	Small, focused team meeting	We collaborated and laughed	Suggest more small-group brainstorms
Task	Designing a new workshop	I love creating from scratch	Offer to create the next team training
Role	Supporting a new hire	Felt like mentoring/ lifting others	Ask to be a buddy for onboarding
Interaction	One-on-one client coaching session	Deep conversation and personal impact	Block more 1:1 sessions instead of group work

After you've filled in the table, look for repeating themes:

- Do certain **tasks** show up more than once?
- Are you energized by **people** or by **solitude**?
- Does your best work happen in the **morning**, or **late at night**?

- What **role** do you tend to step into when you're at your best?

Use your answers as a compass. Because this isn't just about reflection—it's about **building a life around what actually works for you.**

WARNING SIGNS OF ACCIDENTAL LIVING

Here's the thing about not doing this kind of reflective work: nothing *catastrophic* usually happens. The sky doesn't fall. The alarm doesn't blare. No one taps you on the shoulder and says, "Hey, you're moving away from the life you actually want."

Instead, we just... drift.

We go through the motions. We keep our calendars full, our inboxes tidy-ish and our heads down. And slowly—but unmistakably—we slip into **accidental living.**

We stay in roles that don't fit, because they're convenient or familiar. We say yes to things that drain us, because we're good at them or people expect it. We fill our days with tasks, but forget to check whether those tasks actually move us toward joy, impact or purpose.

And then, one day, we wake up and wonder: *How did I get here?*

That's why this chapter matters.

Because *alignment isn't something we stumble into*. It's something we **build**—through awareness, reflection and a thousand micro-decisions that say, "This matters to me. I want more of this."

We can't always quit the job, cancel the obligation or start over from scratch. But we *can* start spotting the patterns. We *can* start saying yes to more of what fuels us—and no to what doesn't.

You don't have to overhaul your life. You just have to stop being a passenger in it.

Let's get back in the driver's seat.

FINAL REFLECTION: REPLICATING WHAT WORKS

You've taken time to dissect a high point in your work or life—a moment when things *clicked*. Now it's time to do something with what you've learned.

Because awareness is just the first step. **Alignment comes from action.** And the good news? It doesn't require a total reinvention. Small, intentional shifts can create powerful ripple effects.

Take a moment to answer these questions:

- How often do my "best day" ingredients show up in my current life? (Daily? Once a week? Not at all lately?)

- What's one aligned element I can intentionally add this month? (Maybe it's more time for creative work, collaborating with someone who energizes you or taking five minutes to reflect before a meeting.)

- What small shift could I make in how I approach my next project, meeting, or task? (Could you bring in more autonomy, curiosity, collaboration or fun?)

You don't have to rebuild your entire life to feel more like yourself. You just have to start noticing what works—and then choose, *on purpose*, to create more of it.

FINAL TAKEAWAY: ALIGNMENT LEAVES CLUES

Here's what I want you to remember: You're not starting from scratch. You already have *evidence* of what lights you up—what energizes you, what feels meaningful, what makes you lose track of time in the best way.

Your best day wasn't a fluke. It was a **blueprint**.

And the more you slow down to study what works, the more you'll begin to recreate those moments—on purpose and more often.

An aligned life doesn't start by chasing happiness. It starts by paying attention to what's already working—**and asking for more of it.** Let's start asking. 🔑

CHAPTER TWELVE

Key: Future Casting

SOMEWHERE ALONG THE way—probably around 2006—we all got handed the same advice: *Just visualize success.*

Think about what you want, put it out into the universe and the universe will deliver.

It was the era of *The Secret*, vision boards and manifesting your dream life by meditating on it long enough. I remember feeling intrigued but also confused. What exactly was I supposed to *visualize*? How was I supposed to conjure an image of success when I didn't even know what it looked like in real life?

Because here's the truth no one talks about: *You can't picture what you've never seen.*

"You have to see it to be it."

That quote from tennis legend Billie Jean King has always stayed with me. And it's right. It's easy to believe in a possibility when someone has already shown you what it looks like—when you've grown up around people doing the thing, wearing the title, living the dream.

But what if you haven't?

What if your whole life has been full of hard-working people who didn't love their jobs? What if you've never met someone who runs their own business, writes a book, leads a company or travels the world with ease? What if your dreams have always felt vague because there's never been a model close enough to feel real?

That's where this chapter begins.

Yes, visualization is powerful. But it only works when it's paired with something deeper than beautiful aesthetics and a quote in fancy script. It works when it's grounded in *emotion*. In *action*. In *alignment*.

This chapter isn't about tricking your brain into wishful thinking. It's about building a bridge between what you *want* and how you *live*—and then walking across it. Starting now.

THE ROLE MODEL GAP

I didn't grow up around entrepreneurs. Or authors. Or people in "corporate" business, really. I knew teachers. Police officers. Farmers. Nurses. Store clerks. Moms who worked in the home. The people in my orbit were good, hardworking, well-intentioned—and most of them looked worn out. They didn't talk about feeling fulfilled in their jobs. They talked about paying bills, staying afloat and getting through the week.

When people told me I could "be anything I wanted," I believed them in theory. But deep down, I didn't know what that meant. Be *what*, exactly? I'd never seen someone run their own business. I didn't know what it looked like to write a book or lead a team or fly off to speak at a conference. Those things weren't just out of reach—they were out of frame entirely. You might as well have told me to become a deep-sea diver on a planet I'd never heard of.

And it turns out I'm not alone.

According to a Gallup-Amazon study, people who had access to *successful career role models* during their youth are significantly more likely to:

- Feel fulfilled in their careers (68% vs. 51%)
- Be in roles where they feel established (64% vs. 45%)
- Earn enough to live comfortably (60% vs. 39%)

That same study found that three in five adults say they received little to no career education in school. No wonder so many of us stumble into jobs without a clear sense of what else might be possible.

The gap is even more pronounced for women and other underrepresented groups. According to GE's research on corporate diversity, one of the *top reasons* women don't rise to leadership roles is a lack of access to role models and mentors in leadership. When there's only one woman at the top for every hundred junior-level women, she becomes a symbol, not a support system. And even when that one woman wants to help, she's often juggling the demands of work, family and everything in between. It's not a lack of willingness—it's a lack of bandwidth.

So what do we do if the path we want doesn't exist in our immediate line of sight? How do we begin to imagine something we've never seen modeled?

That's where **Future Casting** comes in.

It's the practice of borrowing the feelings of a future version of yourself—and then using them to build the road that leads there. Because just because you haven't seen it yet doesn't mean it isn't real.

THE POWER OF VISUALIZATION
(WITH A TWIST)

Let's be honest: the whole visualization thing can sound a little... woowoo.

Close your eyes. Imagine success. Picture yourself in your dream job, your dream house, your dream body, surrounded by joy and abundance. And voilà—life delivers.

Except not really.

I've always been a little skeptical of that version of visualization. It can feel like putting a vision board on a pedestal and hoping the universe picks up your dry cleaning. The idea that simply picturing success will cause it to materialize feels incomplete at best—and dangerously passive at worst.

But here's what I've learned: **visualization isn't about magic. It's about alignment.** Not just imagining things you want, but feeling the emotional and mental state of the person who's already living that life—and then letting that feeling *pull you forward into action*.

I discovered this in an unexpected way while writing this book.

For months, the manuscript felt like a foggy dream. I knew the content mattered. I believed in it. But the end felt so far off. Until I made a simple change.

I had a friend mockup a book cover. Then I printed out a photo of myself *holding* the book—just a Photoshop trick, nothing fancy. I taped it to the wall next to my monitor, where I could see it every single day.

And everything changed.

Suddenly, I wasn't writing toward a vague finish line. I was writing toward *that moment*—the one where I held my book in my hands, where I saw my name on the spine, where someone else read the words and felt seen. I could picture myself signing books at an event, using it in workshops, packing it into client gift boxes. I could feel the energy of that reality. And it lit a fire under me.

It wasn't about *the book*—it was about the sense of contribution, clarity, impact. Seeing it gave me motivation. Feeling it gave me clarity. Believing it made me act. That's the twist: visualization isn't about conjuring castles in the sky. It's about rooting your goals in sensory, emotional truth—and letting that truth guide your next right step.

WHY VISUALIZATION WORKS
(BACKED BY RESEARCH)

The first time I heard the term "visualization" in a non-fluffy, high-stakes context, it was during the Olympics. A reporter was interviewing a downhill skier and asked about his training routine. The skier explained that before each race, he mentally rehearsed every second of the course—closing his eyes and *feeling* the wind in his face, *hearing* the skis cut into the snow and ice, *seeing* the turns ahead as if he were already in motion.

Once I heard that, I started paying attention. Sure enough, before nearly every run, elite skiers would stand at the top of the slope, eyes closed, slightly shifting their bodies, as if they were already racing. They were visualizing—not just hoping to win, but *practicing it in their minds.*

It turns out this isn't just a mindset trick—it's backed by science.

In one well-known study, basketball players were split into three groups to test how mental practice compared to physical practice.

- Group 1 didn't practice at all.
- Group 2 practiced shooting free throws every day for 30 minutes.
- Group 3 spent 30 minutes a day *visualizing* perfect free throws—no physical practice, just mental.

The results?

- Group 1 showed no improvement (no surprise).
- Group 2 improved by 24%.
- Group 3—who never touched a ball—improved by **23%**.

That's nearly identical progress. Just by visualizing. Why does this work?

Maxwell Maltz's classic book *Psycho-Cybernetics* offers one explanation: **your brain doesn't distinguish much between what's real and what's vividly imagined.** It reacts to mental imagery almost the same way it reacts to lived experience. So when you rehearse success, your mind and body begin preparing for that success. Neural pathways are built. Confidence builds. Your actions start to shift.

This isn't just theoretical. Research on Dynamic Neurocognitive Imagery (used in training professional dancers) has found that athletes and performers who incorporate vivid imagery into their practice improve both technical execution and emotional expression.

The bottom line?

Visualization allows you to *practice success before you live it*. It helps you create a roadmap not just for what you want to do, but for who you're becoming.

And that's where things start to get powerful.

TWO KINDS OF VISUALIZATION THAT WORK

Not all visualization is created equal. Over time, I've discovered that there are two distinct types, and both serve different but powerful purposes.

1. POSITIVE VISUALIZATION

This is the classic form: you see yourself *winning*. Not just the surface-level dream, but the *feelings* that come with it.

For me, one of the most powerful positive visualizations was imagining myself coming home from the gym. In the scene I created in my mind, I'd just finished a great workout. I felt strong, my cheeks were flushed, my body was energized but relaxed. I stepped into the house and caught my reflection in the hallway mirror—not picking apart my flaws but smiling with pride and ease. I visualized myself fitting comfortably into my clothes, walking with confidence, breathing deeper.

It wasn't about picturing a specific number on the scale. It was about capturing the feeling of **alignment**—pride, vitality, capability. That vision pulled me forward, day after day, when motivation alone would have failed.

2. DEDUCTIVE VISUALIZATION

This one doesn't get talked about as much—but it's equally important. Deductive visualization is about mentally *rehearsing the hard parts*. The potential derailers. The moments that used to trip you up.

Example: Dessert at a restaurant with friends. Historically, I struggled to say no when everyone around me was ordering something indulgent and urging me to do the same. I LOVE sugary, creamy desserts. But I also wanted to be healthier and make more positive food decisions.

So, I visualized it.

I pictured myself at the table. I imagined the smells, the menu being passed around, the moment a friend said, "Let's just get a few to share!" I felt the awkward pause, the temptation, the internal tug-of-war... and then I imagined myself smiling, declining and *surviving* the moment. I felt the pride afterward. I visualized walking out of the restaurant still feeling good in my body. Not deprived—*empowered*.

Deductive visualization is about preparing for resistance and reminding yourself that you can handle it. It builds emotional muscle memory.

WHY YOU NEED BOTH

Positive visualization shows you where you're going—and how good it will feel when you get there. Deductive visualization prepares you for what might try to pull you off course—and how you'll navigate it with grace.

Use them together. Picture the win. Practice the challenge. Watch your reality shift.

HOW TO USE VISUALIZATION IN REAL LIFE

So how do you actually *do* visualization—not as a vague intention or Pinterest dream board, but as a real, transformative practice? Here's a step-by-step approach that's worked powerfully for me:

1. WRITE IT LIKE A MOVIE SCENE

Don't just think in bullet points—*write* your visualization out in vivid, sensory-rich detail. Imagine it like a scene in a film:

- What are you wearing?
- What does the air smell like?
- What's the weather doing?
- What expression is on your face?
- What emotion is pulsing through your body?

The more specific, the better. Include sounds, physical sensations, even dialogue. Your brain doesn't respond to vague goals—it responds to *experience*.

2. MAKE IT DAILY (JUST A FEW MINUTES)

You don't need hours. You need intention. Once you've written the scene, close your eyes and *live it* for 3-5 minutes a day. Morning, night—whenever you'll be least interrupted.

Think of it as mental rehearsal. You're training your mind and body to recognize success as familiar, not foreign.

3. EXPECT RESISTANCE

At first, your brain might rebel. The vision will feel fuzzy. Your inner critic will pipe up. You'll forget what you were picturing halfway through. All of that is *normal*.

You're building a new neural pathway. It takes repetition, not perfection.

4. KEEP PRACTICING—THE VIVIDNESS WILL GROW

Every time you revisit the vision, it will get clearer. You'll be able to drop into it faster. Eventually, it becomes part of how you *see* yourself—which directly influences how you *show up*.

And here's the part I didn't fully believe until I saw it work: behavior begins to follow.

HERE'S WHAT SHIFTED FOR ME:

- I visualized myself turning down desserts at restaurants—then started doing it with ease in real life.
- I visualized walking past junk food at the store and leaving it on the shelf—and found it was no longer calling to me.
- I visualized myself sitting at my computer, focused and productive instead of doomscrolling—and slowly, my writing habits transformed.
- I visualized my book in my hands, on a stage, being talked about—and now, I'm writing this with a cover mockup taped to my wall.

Visualization isn't magic. It's *practice*. And like any practice, it gets stronger the more you show up. So start small. Write one scene. Play it in your mind for a few days. Watch what begins to shift.

REFLECTION ACTIVITY: VISION MAPPING, THE TACTILE WAY

This is where we make the abstract tangible. Sometimes, getting your hands involved helps your brain and body connect to the vision in a different way.

INSTRUCTIONS:

1. **Gather your materials:**
   Grab a stack of old magazines, catalogs, travel brochures, junk mail, printed photos, even torn-up packaging or postcards. You can also print things you find online.

2. **Flip and feel:**
   Without overthinking, flip through the pages and cut out anything that *pulls you in*. Don't try to make it make sense. You're not curating an Instagram-perfect board here. You're letting your intuition speak.
   - Images
   - Words or phrases

- Colors, patterns or textures
- Symbols or objects

3. Assemble your board:

Paste your cutouts onto a blank sheet of paper, poster board or inside a journal spread. Let it take whatever shape it wants. There's no "right" layout—just what feels natural to you.

No editing allowed: This is a judgment-free zone. Don't worry if your board looks random or messy. That's often where the good stuff hides. The goal is to *discover*—not design something polished.

4. After you finish, reflect:

- What themes or patterns emerge? Do you notice a particular energy, color, or feeling that shows up more than once?
- Are there words or images that repeat? Pay attention to any language or visuals your subconscious keeps reaching for.
- Are any of these elements already in your life? Sometimes we're already living part of the dream—we just haven't named it yet.
- What do they suggest about where you're headed?
- Is there a next chapter quietly asking for your attention?

This activity isn't about planning every step. It's about *getting in touch* with what your body and creative instincts already know—and giving your future vision a shape you can see and feel.

Let it guide your next brave steps forward.

MINI REFLECTION: VISUALIZE A SPECIFIC MOMENT

Let's narrow the lens. Instead of collaging an entire future, this reflection helps you zoom in on **one vivid, meaningful moment** you'd love to experience. Not a far-off fantasy—something personal, specific and possible.

PROMPT:
Choose a future moment that matters to you. One that feels like a turning point, a culmination or a celebration. Examples might include:

- Turning in your manuscript
- Getting a promotion
- Launching your business
- Speaking on stage at a conference
- Celebrating a major health milestone
- Signing your first client
- Hearing someone say, "You helped me."

Close your eyes and bring that moment to life. Then, re-flect and write:

- What are you wearing?
  (Be specific—your brain loves detail.)
- Who's there?
  (Friends? Colleagues? Strangers? Just you?)
- What's the energy of the room?
  (Buzzing? Focused? Quiet? Warm?)
- What emotions are you feeling in your body?
  (Pride? Calm? Excitement? Relief? Confidence?)
- What did it take to get here?
  (What habits, choices, risks, or support made this possible?)

This moment is your internal North Star. The more clearly you can see it, the more confidently you can move toward it. Come back to it often. Let it evolve. Let it guide you.

IF YOU CAN FEEL IT, YOU CAN BUILD IT

You don't need the full blueprint yet. You don't have to map every step or know exactly how it'll unfold. The first and most powerful thing you can do is this: **Get emotionally and physically familiar with what aligned success feels like.**

Not just what it looks like on paper—but what it feels like in your chest, your breath, your body. Let that vision live inside you. Let it become familiar. Let it shape your decisions before it becomes your reality.

Because if you can feel it, you can build it.

So here's your challenge: **Try this tangible visualization for two weeks.** Just a few minutes each day. No pressure, no perfection. Then, watch what starts to shift—your habits, your mindset, your energy, your choices.

You might be surprised by how quickly your life starts moving in the direction of what you've been practicing. Remember: *Your mind rehearses before your life catches up. Visualize the life that fits—and then walk toward it.* ⛷

CHAPTER THIRTEEN

Key: Somatic Body Responses

YOU KNOW THAT moment when something feels wrong before you can explain why? Maybe it's a tightening in your stomach, a jaw that won't unclench, a sudden urge to leave a room. Or the opposite—a warmth in your chest, a spark of excitement, a deep sense of calm that washes over you like a wave. You might not have had the words for it right away, but your body knew. Long before your brain sorted out what was happening, your body was already raising its hand saying, *Hey, something's up.*

This isn't woowoo. It's biology.

Our nervous systems are wired to scan for safety and danger, truth and dissonance, alignment and misalignment. Long before our conscious minds weigh the pros and cons or make the to-do list, our bodies are reading the room, reading the energy, reading the *truth*.

As Dr. Bessel van der Kolk says in *The Body Keeps the Score*, our bodies hold on to trauma, memory and emotion in ways we're just beginning to understand. And Dr. Martha Beck's "Shackles On / Shackles Off" framework gives us a simple but powerful way to decode what our bodies are trying to tell us. A shackles-on feeling is contraction, dread, anxiety, heaviness. A shackles-off feeling is lightness, openness, ease, even if it's scary.

Here's the part no one taught us: these physical responses are *information*. They're not random quirks or signs of weakness. They're signals. Like lights on a dashboard, they show us where something needs attention, where something might be off—or exactly right.

This chapter is about learning to read those signals. It's about tuning into the wisdom your body already holds and using it as a compass for alignment. We'll look at real-life examples, walk through reflection exercises and help you start noticing your own patterns.

Because your body has been speaking all along. It's time we started listening.

THE WISDOM OF THE BODY

Somatic responses are your body's way of processing what's happening—often before you're fully aware of it. These are the signals that show up as a tight chest, a gut feeling, jaw tension, shallow breath, warmth, goosebumps or a wave of calm.

They're physical responses that originate in the body, not the brain's logic center.

This isn't just intuition or sensitivity—it's science. Somatic responses are driven by the parts of your brain responsible for survival: the limbic system and the vagus nerve, which together help regulate your nervous system. These areas assess safety and danger automatically, long before the prefrontal cortex—the rational, logical part of your brain—can weigh in.

Think of it this way: your body is a high-speed surveillance system. It gathers and processes information about your environment, your relationships and your choices faster than your conscious mind can even catch up. It's not always neat or convenient, but it's incredibly wise.

So when your stomach drops as you walk into a room, or you suddenly feel energized around a new idea—don't dismiss it. That's your body giving you data. When I was working with that state agency who had the leadership change, my body knew the changes weren't for the better. It was my brain that took a minute to catch up.

Here's the most important truth I can offer you in this chapter: *Your body is not betraying you. It's informing you.*

REFLECTION EXERCISE:
WHAT IS YOUR BODY TRYING TO TELL YOU?

Your body has been sending you signals for years—you may have just learned to tune them out, override them or rationalize them away. This exercise is about tuning back in. Grab your journal or a blank page and reflect on the following:

1. WHEN I'M ANXIOUS OR OVERWHELMED, WHAT PHYSICAL SIGNALS SHOW UP?

Think about moments when you felt dread, panic or deep stress. What happened in your body?

- Did your jaw clench during high-pressure work environments?
- Did your stomach tighten or churn?
- Did your breathing get shallow or your shoulders climb toward your ears?
- Did your body develop a rash, like hives?
- Did you feel nauseated, overheated, faint or frozen?

List **3–5 real experiences** where your body responded to stress, even before your brain could name it.

2. WHEN I'M IN FLOW, ALIGNMENT OR PEACE, WHAT DOES MY BODY FEEL LIKE?

Recall times when you felt calm, inspired, joyful or truly grounded.

- Did you sleep more deeply?
- Smile so much your cheeks ached?
- Get bursts of energy or creativity?
- Feel a warm chest, steady breath, open posture or quiet mind?
- Did time fly in a good way?

Write down **3–5 real examples** when your body clearly signaled alignment.

Then step back and ask yourself:

- What patterns do I see?
- Are there early warning signs I usually ignore?
- What does my version of "shackles on" or "shackles off" look like in my body?

Your body has been telling the truth this whole time. Now's your chance to start listening.

THE JAW THAT LOCKED

I didn't know, when I was a child and curled up in the backseat of our car on the way to the hospital, that my jaw was trying to tell me something.

It had locked shut. Not metaphorically—literally. My mom had tried warm compresses, gentle coaxing, maybe some

Tylenol. Nothing worked. I couldn't open my mouth. The pain was excruciating and we had no idea what was happening. So off we went, scared and uncertain, until a very large orthopedic doctor used what can only be described as sheer force to get it open.

Ouch.

The diagnosis? TMJ. Temporomandibular joint disorder. The consensus was that it must be a dental issue—something about tooth alignment or jaw structure. Orthodontia would fix it. I was "cleared" to go home.

What nobody asked, and what I didn't have words for back then, was this: *What else was happening in your life when this started?*

Because the truth is, I wasn't just a kid with a tricky jaw. I was a kid living in a house filled with fear. My father had a hair-trigger temper. I never knew what would set him off, only that when it happened, it would end in violence. My mom and I were scared of him, every single day. I was regularly hit and spanked so hard I would wet my pants. I learned quickly that crying only made it worse (my father's favorite saying was "stop crying or I'll give you something to cry about"), so I became skilled at the "quiet cry"—the one where your body shakes but no sound comes out. I didn't even realize, at the time, how much tension I held in my body just to survive.

Of course my jaw locked. It was doing what it had always done: hold it in, clamp it down, survive without making a sound.

What's wild is that this didn't stop when the immediate danger did. Even after my mom found the courage to kick him out—something I still marvel at—my body kept the score. The TMJ issues would show up later in school, during times of high stress or perceived threat. Like during marching band practice in the sweltering Texas heat, where the director would scream, punch kids in the stomach (he claimed it only hurt if we weren't breathing right) and humiliate us in front of our peers. The old fear came rushing back. The jaw would start to ache. Sometimes it would pop. Sometimes it would lock.

I thought it was just a weird recurring thing. Something unfortunate, sure, but explainable by stress or genetics or bad posture. It took me years to understand that it wasn't random at all. It was my body saying: *"This feels familiar. This feels unsafe."*

Connecting those dots changed everything. Suddenly, my body wasn't betraying me. It was **informing** me. It had always been trying to say something—I just didn't know how to listen yet.

We all have something like this. A recurring headache that always hits around certain people. A stomach that knots before opening the inbox. A rash that flares when the to-do list gets too long. Our bodies speak in symptoms. And when we finally start tracing those signals back to their source, what we uncover isn't weakness—it's wisdom.

FEAR IN THE BOARDROOM – THE HIVES JOB

On paper, it sounded amazing. A recruiter friend reached out with what she framed as a once-in-a-career opportunity: a pre-IPO tech startup needed a VP of HR to get them ready for launch. I could make a big impact, help shape the future of the company and—if all went to plan—walk away in 18 months with a huge payday after they went public.

It wasn't what I was looking for. I had my own business. I loved the work I was doing. But the offer was shiny, promising, lucrative. I convinced myself it could be a smart detour. My husband and I talked it over and together we decided I should go for it. "It's just 18 months," I said. "We'll treat it like a cash play."

But here's the truth: **My body knew from day one that something wasn't right.**

Even during the interview process, there were red flags. The energy in the office felt... off. The employees looked tense. The CEO talked about himself nonstop and barely asked me any questions. The commute was over an hour each way. None of it felt good. And yet, I rationalized every piece of it away. I saw the signs and told myself they didn't matter.

Because I was there for the money. I could endure anything for 18 months, right?

On my very first day, the dissonance slammed into me. People I'd never met lined up outside my door to complain. The CEO dragged me off to tour new office space—news to me, by the way, that the office was moving—and then demanded that I run an impromptu executive meeting. When I didn't immediately take charge, he launched into a profanity-laced tirade about how stupid and useless his employees were. I sat there stunned.

That night, my family had prepared a special dinner to celebrate my new role. I walked in the door, smiled and then burst into tears. I couldn't eat. My stomach was in knots. I told myself to get it together.

So I did what so many of us are taught to do: I pushed through. I slapped a smile on my face. I repeated my new mantra: *18 months, 18 months, 18 months.*

By the end of week four, I was covered in red, angry welts. Head to toe. It started as a faint itch, then got worse. At first, I blamed our laundry detergent. Then maybe a new, weird food allergy. But when my husband walked in, took one look at me soaking in an oatmeal bath, and said "Oh my god, you have hives," I couldn't ignore it anymore.

We Googled hives and discovered that when people are under stress for long periods of time, it triggers a cortisol immune response in the body.

I was literally allergic to my job.

My body knew what my brain was still trying to deny.

Once I finally admitted it—this wasn't a temporary rough patch, this wasn't a grit-your-teeth season, this was *fundamentally misaligned*—everything got clearer. I gave my notice. The CEO reacted exactly as you'd expect: angry, narcissistic, insulting. And still, I walked out that door.

Within 48 hours, the hives were gone.

Here's the kicker: that company never went public. It folded.

I didn't miss out on a golden opportunity—I narrowly escaped a disaster. But more importantly, I learned this: **when your body starts screaming, it's time to listen.** What starts as feathers (tension, irritability, fatigue) becomes hammers (illness, breakdown, full-system revolt) if you ignore it long enough.

And I had ignored it long enough.

REFLECTION EXERCISE: THE SOMATIC SIGNAL MAP

One of the most powerful ways to understand your alignment (or lack of it) is to learn the unique language your body speaks. This exercise will help you begin to track how your emotional states show up physically—because your body is always giving you information, even when your brain isn't ready to hear it.

Use the chart below to fill in your own somatic signals as they relate to different emotional states. You can use the examples provided as a starting point, but don't feel limited by them. This is about your body's patterns—not anyone else's.

EMOTIONAL STATE	PHYSICAL SIGNAL
Stress / Overwhelm	e.g. Tight jaw, clenched fists, shallow breathing
Joy / Alignment	e.g. Open chest, warm face, increased energy
Dread / Avoidance	e.g. Stomach knots, headaches, urge to procrastinate

EMOTIONAL STATE	PHYSICAL SIGNAL
Excitement / Flow	e.g. Sparkling eyes, upright posture, "buzzing" energy
Grief / Sadness	e.g. Heaviness in chest, fatigue, teary eyes

PROMPT:

Start paying attention to what your body feels like in real-time during your day. When something stressful happens, where does that tension go? When you feel energized or joyful, what changes physically?

ASK YOURSELF:

- Which physical signals seem to show up the most?
- Are there certain emotions you tend to ignore or numb out?
- What patterns are emerging from your body's cues?

This is a tool you can return to over and over. The more fluent you become in reading your body's signals, the faster you'll be able to recognize misalignment—and move toward what brings you back to center.

IGNORING THE FEATHERS –
THE KIDNEY STONE WAKE-UP

Here's the thing about ignoring your body's gentle nudges: it doesn't stop nudging. It just gets louder. What starts as a feather—a little tension, a skipped meal, a restless night—can escalate into a hammer if left unchecked. And in my case? That hammer took the form of a kidney stone.

At the time, I was doing *all* the things. I had my own business and, like most entrepreneurs in the early stages, I wore every hat: trainer, coach, bookkeeper, social media manager, travel planner, tech support, invoice tracker, client wrangler. And on top of that? I was newly remarried, with bonus kids and all the life chaos that comes with blending families. But I didn't think twice. I kept juggling, telling myself this was just the grind phase—that things would settle down eventually.

Spoiler: they didn't.

One Friday, I was on a client call in my home office when something shifted. Fast. I suddenly felt nauseous and made an excuse to hang up. Seconds later, I was throwing up and doubled over on the floor in blinding pain. It hit like a freight train. My first instinct wasn't to call 911 or even my husband. Instead, I started *problem-solving*. Could I crawl to the garage and drive myself to urgent care between pain waves? Could I wait for my husband to get off work and drive an hour home? Was there *anyone* I could call who wouldn't be inconvenienced?

Welcome to the mind of someone who's spent a lifetime idolizing self-reliance. The idea of asking for help—*really* asking—felt harder than the pain.

Eventually, I called my college-age daughter. She was working as a nanny at the time, but she dropped everything (don't worry—she found coverage for the kids) and raced over. When she walked in, I was crumpled on the floor, covered in vomit and crying uncontrollably. Not exactly my usual Superwoman aesthetic.

As she drove me to the ER, I was panting and told her I had three clients waiting on deliverables. Between contractions of pain, I was dictating who she should contact and what she should say. She took my phone, assured me she had it covered and told me to stop worrying. One of the clients, a VP at a major company, was named Sara. I stressed how important it was to notify her.

Fast forward to Monday when I saw a message from Sara asking where her project was.

Wait—hadn't that been handled?

I asked my daughter how she contacted Sara. With total confidence she replied, "I texted her."

Here's the kicker: I *didn't* have Sara's cell number. The only number saved was her landline—her corporate office phone. My Gen Z daughter had unknowingly sent a desperate emergency text to a desk phone... that probably blinked red for a week before anyone noticed. I laughed (then cried), because it was such a perfect metaphor for how disconnected I had become. I thought I was communicating clearly, managing it all. But I was sending SOS signals to the wrong places—just like I was doing with my own body.

It turns out, I had a massive kidney stone brought on by extreme dehydration and prolonged stress.

The bigger truth was that this didn't come out of nowhere. My body had been whispering for weeks. I'd just ignored every feather: the skipped meals, the short temper, the fatigue, the mystery pain in my lower back. Until it sent a hammer.

After I recovered, I made real changes. I hired help. I built systems. I stopped pretending I was fine. Because the lesson was crystal clear: Extreme self-reliance got me into this. Somatic wisdom helped get me out.

MINI-REFLECTION: MY EARLIEST PHYSICAL WARNING SIGNS

Let's bring this into the now. You've heard my stories—but what about yours?

Take a moment to reflect on how your body tries to get your attention when something's off. Not when it's a full-blown crisis, but in the early stages—when the feathers are still soft and subtle.

Ask yourself:

- What's the *first* physical sign that I'm pushing too hard? (Is it tension in your shoulders? A dull headache? Snapping at people you love?)
- When did I *last ignore* that signal—and what happened next?

- What would it look like to *respect* that signal instead? (Maybe you pause. Cancel something. Take a nap. Drink water. Say no.)

These moments matter. Your body isn't trying to slow you down out of spite—it's trying to protect you. Start paying attention to the whispers before they become shouts.

YOUR BODY IS A COMPASS

If you've ever felt a pit in your stomach walking into a room—or a strange sense of peace about a choice that didn't make logical sense—you've already experienced what Dr. Martha Beck, an author, life coach, speaker and sociologist, calls "shackles on/shackles off."

It's a simple practice, but incredibly powerful once you start using it regularly. Here's the gist:

- **Shackles On** = constriction, tension, dread.
  Your body might tighten, your breathing might get shallow, you feel heavy or boxed in. This is your nervous system whispering *nope, not for me.*

- **Shackles Off** = expansion, ease, lightness.
  You feel like your chest opens, your energy lifts or

there's a sudden sense of calm. *This is your internal compass pointing to alignment.*

You don't need a quiet room or meditation mat to use this. Try it on everyday decisions:

- Say the option out loud: "Take on this client."
- Then pause and scan your body. Do you feel tight or light? Tense or open?
- Try another: "Say no to that opportunity."
- Again, scan. What does your chest say? Your gut? Your jaw?

Over time, this becomes a loop you can trust. Your body knows before your brain does—and it doesn't lie.

This isn't about magic. It's about biology. It's about finally recognizing that your body is wired to protect you, to guide you, to keep you aligned. You just have to start listening.

REFLECTION EXERCISE: THE SHACKLES TEST

Let's try this in real time.

1. **Choose a decision you're currently considering.**
   It can be big ("Should I take that job?") or small
   ("Should I commit to that dinner invitation on Friday?").

2. **Sit quietly for a moment.**
   Let your shoulders drop. Unclench your jaw. Take a few
   slow breaths to bring your awareness into your body.

3. **Now, imagine saying YES to that decision.**
   Say it aloud if it helps: "Yes, I'll do it."
   - What happens in your body?
   - Do you feel tightness, heaviness, a sense of dread—
     or lightness, openness, ease?

4. **Now, imagine saying NO.**
   Say: "No, I'm not doing it."
   - What changes physically?
   - What does your breath do? What about your
     shoulders, your chest, your stomach?

5. **Journal your responses.**
   - Which answer felt like "shackles off"?
   - What did your body want you to know?
   - Are there subtle patterns you notice when some-
     thing is aligned vs. misaligned?

Remember: this isn't about finding the "perfect" answer. It's about learning to hear the signals your body's already sending. You don't need to force it. Just notice.

NORMALIZING SOMATIC AWARENESS

If all of this feels a little unfamiliar—or even a little uncomfortable—you're not alone. Many of us were never taught to pay attention to our bodies in this way. In fact, some of us were actively trained to ignore them.

Especially for trauma survivors, tuning in to the body can feel confusing or even threatening. When your body has been a site of stress, fear or pain, it makes perfect sense that you'd distance yourself from its signals. And if you've spent years pushing through discomfort, overriding your needs or "being the strong one," it may take some time to relearn how to listen.

That's okay.

Somatic awareness isn't a switch—it's a skill. One that develops over time with compassion and curiosity, not judgment. There's no behind. There's no "too late." This isn't a race.

Somatic literacy is just like any other language. You're not late. You're learning.

Start simple. Ask questions like:

- Where do I feel tension when I'm overwhelmed?

- What happens in my body when I'm excited?
- What's my first physical signal that something is off?

And then listen—not with urgency or pressure, but with kindness. Your body has always been talking. Now, you're just beginning to hear what it has to say.

MINI REFLECTION: WHAT HAVE I BEEN TRAINED TO IGNORE?

Take a quiet moment with this one. These aren't surface-level questions—they're invitations to gently peel back what you've learned and start rewriting the script.

Ask yourself:

- Did my family growing up make space for emotions, or dismiss them as weakness or drama?

- Was I praised more for powering through than for paying attention to my needs?

- What somatic signals (tight chest, clenching jaw, exhaustion, etc.) did I learn to override or explain away? Now pause and name one.

What is one signal your body sends that you want to stop dismissing? Write it down. Let this be your permission slip to start noticing—and honoring—it.

YOUR BODY IS ON YOUR SIDE

If you take one thing from this chapter, let it be this: your body is not working against you. The tension, the headaches, the nausea, the fatigue—these aren't random malfunctions or inconveniences to push through. They're signals. Clues. Tiny messengers with important things to say.

You may have been trained to override them. You may have learned that discomfort means you're weak or that listening to your body makes you unreliable. But the truth is exactly the opposite.

Your body wants alignment. It wants peace. It wants truth. And it will speak in a whisper or a roar to get your attention.

What if, instead of ignoring those signals or shaming yourself for having them, you got curious? What if you learned to treat your body like a trusted ally—a wise companion pointing you back to what matters?

Because here's the thing: The more you listen, the sooner you'll hear. The sooner you hear, the sooner you'll know. And when you know—then you can choose. 🔑

CHAPTER FOURTEEN

Key: Ultradian Rhythms

LET'S START WITH a truth that might feel like heresy in the corporate world: you were never meant to be productive from 8:00 AM to 5:00 p.m or beyond. Not continuously. Not without pause.

And certainly not with a smile plastered on your face while your inbox eats you alive.

But that's the story we've been sold. That a "good" employee, a "serious" entrepreneur or a "high-performing" leader is someone who powers through—who ignores the yawn, pushes past the fog and keeps grinding even when their brain has clearly left the building. Somewhere along the way, exhaustion became a badge of honor. "I'm slammed," we say, like it's something to be proud of. We celebrate the late nights, the skipped lunches, the always-on availability. We mistake burnout for commitment.

And when we can't keep up? When we find ourselves staring at a screen, unable to focus or string together a sentence, we assume the problem must be us.

You're not broken. You're not lazy. You're not undisciplined.

You're human. And humans move in waves—biologically, cognitively, emotionally. Your energy was never meant to be one flat line of constant output. It was designed to rise and fall, to crest and crash, to cycle through bursts of clarity and pockets of recovery.

This chapter is about learning to work with those rhythms—not against them. Because the key to aligned productivity isn't in pushing harder. It's in paying attention to when you actually have something to give—and then organizing your life to honor that truth.

RHYTHMS BEFORE ROUTINES

Long before we had color-coded calendars and calendar alerts, human beings lived by a different kind of schedule—one written in sunlight and seasons. In agrarian and Indigenous cultures, people rose with the sun, worked in focused bursts, paused for rest and shifted their activity depending on the weather, harvest cycle and how their bodies felt. Rest wasn't a reward—it was a rhythm. Productivity ebbed and flowed, just like everything else in nature.

Then came the Industrial Age and with it, a new set of expectations. Machines didn't rest, so workers weren't supposed to either. The goal was continuous output, not creativity. Standardization and efficiency became the gold standard and suddenly the eight-hour (or more!) workday was born—not because it made sense for the human body, but because it made sense for factory lines.

Fast-forward to today and many of us are still operating on that outdated template. We show up, stay alert and try to produce in rigid, uniform blocks of time—ignoring how we actually feel in the name of being "productive."

But here's the truth: the 8-hour workday wasn't built for your biology. It was built for machines. And you, thankfully, are not a machine.

THE SCIENCE BEHIND THE WAVES

In his book *When*, Daniel Pink lays out a compelling truth that many of us intuitively know but rarely acknowledge: "Our cognitive abilities do not remain static over the course of the day. They change—in predictable and sometimes extreme ways." In other words, your brain doesn't stay equally sharp from morning to night. It pulses. Peaks. Dips. Recovers. And then starts again.

That pulse is driven by something called **ultradian rhythms**—natural cycles of energy and focus that repeat every 90 to 120 minutes. During each cycle, your body and brain rise into a period of high alertness and performance, followed by a dip when your system begins calling for rest and renewal.

It's why you might find yourself crushing it mid-morning, only to feel foggy or distracted an hour and a half later. That dip isn't a flaw. It's not a sign that you lack discipline or drive. It's your body's internal clock doing exactly what it's designed to do—asking you to pause, breathe, stretch, walk, nap, eat or simply reset.

Most people cycle through one to three strong ultradian rhythms each day. If we tune into those natural waves and learn to work *with* them instead of against them, we can unlock a more sustainable kind of productivity—one that honors our biology instead of constantly overriding it.

WHAT HAPPENS WHEN WE IGNORE THE SIGNALS

Most of us have been taught to override our body's cues. Push through. Stay focused. Hustle harder. But the truth is, when we ignore our natural rhythms, our productivity—and our well-being—start to suffer.

The signs of rhythm resistance are everywhere. You might feel foggy by mid-afternoon, reaching for caffeine or sugar to jolt yourself back to life. Or maybe you power through the day checking off dozens of small tasks, only to realize at 6 PM that you didn't touch the one thing on your To Do List that actually mattered. That feeling of being "busy but behind" isn't a time management issue—it's a misalignment between your energy and your effort.

I once worked with a brilliant VP at a Fortune 500 company who was constantly overwhelmed. Her days were packed with meetings, emails and urgent requests. When I asked her, "When do you do your actual work?" she blinked and said, "After my kids go to bed."

Let that sink in. She was doing her most critical thinking and decision-making *after 9 PM*, when her brain and body were already depleted. No wonder she was burned out.

This is what happens when we don't align our work with our energy. We end up giving our clearest thinking to inbox zero and our foggiest hours to strategy. We spend our peak windows in reactive mode and our creative work—if we get to it at all—gets whatever scraps are left.

We don't need to work harder. We need to work *with ourselves*, not against ourselves.

Because your best energy deserves your best work.

BRAVERY LOOKS LIKE BLOCKING TIME

When we think of bravery at work, we often picture bold speeches, hard conversations or taking big risks. But sometimes, bravery is quieter—and far more personal. Sometimes, it looks like blocking off two hours on your calendar and refusing to let it be filled. It looks like protecting your best energy for your most meaningful work.

I once coached a high-level leader who was brilliant, respected and completely overwhelmed. Her calendar was a wall of back-to-back meetings from 7:30 AM to 6:00 PM, and she regularly worked nights to get her real work done. When I asked her when she had time to think—*really* think—she hesitated. Then she admitted, "I don't."

Together, we looked at her energy rhythms and noticed that her clearest, most focused hours were mid-morning. So we made a small but powerful change: she started blocking 9:00 to 11:00 AM for deep work. At first, she was nervous—worried that people would see her as uncooperative or unavailable. But something amazing happened: her impact skyrocketed. Not because she worked more, but because she worked *smarter*—doing the right things at the right time.

This is what energy-aligned bravery looks like. And it doesn't have to be dramatic. Microbrave acts make a big difference:

- Asking if a 30-minute meeting can be done in 15.
- Skipping a meeting you don't need to attend (and just reading the recap).
- Saying no to "just a quick call" that cuts into your peak energy window.
- Blocking your calendar with a simple "Focus Time" and treating it as sacred.

You don't need permission to honor your energy. You need clarity—and courage.

Because when you protect your best hours, you protect your best work. And that's brave.

MYTHS THAT KEEP US STUCK

We live in a culture that treats burnout like a rite of passage and busy like a status symbol. Somewhere along the line, we started equating productivity with worthiness. The busier you are, the more valuable you must be—right? That's the myth. And it's costing us dearly.

Let's break down some of the most common productivity lies we've been taught:

MYTH #1: "BUSY MEANS SUCCESSFUL."

We've glorified hustle so thoroughly that simply being in motion—regardless of direction—has become its own kind of achievement. But activity is not the same as impact. Just because your calendar is full doesn't mean your life is. True success isn't measured by how much you can cram into a day—it's measured by how much of what you're doing actually matters to you. Being "busy" might feel like progress, but if it's not aligned with your purpose, it's just noise.

MYTH #2: "REST IS LAZY."

Rest has been unfairly framed as indulgent, optional or even weak. But here's the truth: your brain and body aren't designed to operate at full speed all day. Rest isn't something you earn after pushing yourself to the edge—it's a biological necessity. When you deny yourself rest, you're not being a hero. You're sabotaging your capacity to show up fully. Rested people are sharper, more creative, more resilient. Rest is fuel, not failure.

MYTH #3: "YOU JUST NEED MORE WILLPOWER."

If you've ever hit an afternoon slump and told yourself to "push through," you've met this myth head-on. Willpower, it turns out, is a finite resource. It's like a muscle that tires with overuse. And if you're trying to white-knuckle your way through every task, you're not optimizing your time—you're draining yourself. It's not about gritting your teeth and going harder. It's about working smarter, with your natural rhythms, not against them.

Arianna Huffington, in her book *Thrive*, said it best: *"Burnout is not the price you have to pay for success."*

And yet, so many of us are still writing the check.

We've been sold a model of success that requires us to abandon ourselves—our rest, our well-being, our humanity—in favor of constant output. But that model is broken. And it's time to stop buying into it.

Here's the reframe we need: **Rest is not a reward. It's a strategy.**

It's the most intelligent, most effective way to sustain creativity, focus and long-term performance. It's how you protect the very resource that drives everything else—your energy.

Think of it this way: you wouldn't run your phone on 1% battery and expect it to function at full capacity. Yet we do this to ourselves every day. The goal isn't to work more. It's to work in rhythm with your body, your brain, your biology.

And when we start treating rest as part of the plan—instead of the escape after everything else is done—we stop surviving our days and start designing lives that actually work.

DISCOVERING YOUR RHYTHM

So how do you begin working *with* your body instead of against it? You map the waves. You learn your natural rhythm.

While most of us have been trained to plan our schedules based on external demands—meeting invites, school drop-off times, deadlines—few of us have ever been taught to organize our work around our energy. But that's exactly what ultradian rhythms invite us to do.

Here's a simple, science-backed process to help you discover your personal productivity curve:

STEP 1: TRACK YOUR ENERGY EVERY 90 MINUTES FOR A WEEK

Set a recurring timer or calendar alert every 90 minutes throughout your workday. Each time it goes off, jot down how you're feeling in that moment. Don't overthink it—just a quick check-in will do.

Are you sharp? Fuzzy? Focused? Distracted? Sluggish? Buzzing with ideas? Ready for a nap?

It may feel a bit annoying at first, but give it a few days. What you're doing is collecting data—real feedback from your body, not just assumptions from your brain.

STEP 2: SPOT YOUR PERSONAL PEAK, DIP AND REBOUND

At the end of the week, review your notes. What trends emerge?

- When are you naturally most focused?
- When does your attention start to drift?
- Is there a second wind later in the day?
- When does your mood typically crash?

Most people have one to three strong ultradian cycles during the day. These show up as roughly 90-minute windows of clarity, followed by dips where the body begs for a reset. No two people are exactly alike, but patterns almost always show up if you're willing to look.

STEP 3: MATCH TASK TYPES TO ENERGY ZONES
Now that you've got some insight, it's time to use it.

- **Use your peaks** for deep work—writing, planning, problem-solving, strategic thinking.
- **Use your dips** for low-stakes or automatic tasks— emails, data entry, admin, errands.
- **Use your rebounds** (those second wind windows) for creative work—brainstorming, designing, collaborative conversations.

This is the moment your calendar becomes a tool for energy alignment—not just time management. It's where your effectiveness starts to multiply, not because you're doing more, but because you're doing things *at the right time*.

USE A SIMPLE LOG TO MAKE IT EASY

You can jot your check-ins in a notebook or download the free Energy Rhythm Log I've linked to on www.alifealignedbook. com. Here's a basic version of what to include:

- **Time** of day
- **Energy level** (High / Medium / Low)
- **Clarity** (Sharp / Foggy / Distracted)

- **Mood** (Calm / Irritable / Happy / Flat / Restless)
- **What you were doing** (Task or activity)

SAMPLE LOG FORMAT

TIME	ENERGY LEVEL (High / Medium / Low)	CLARITY (Sharp / Foggy / Distracted)	MOOD	ACTIVITY
9:00 AM	High	Sharp	Calm	Writing client proposal
10:30 AM	Medium	Starting to draft	Tense	In Zoom meeting
12:00 PM	Low	Foggy	Irritable	Email catch-up
1:30 PM	Medium	Clearer	Neutral	Lunch & admin tasks
3:00 pm	High	Creative	Energized	Brainstorming session

Over time, this becomes your personal road map—clear, honest and unique to you. You don't need to overhaul your whole life to benefit from this. Even a small shift—like moving your hardest task to your natural focus window—can change the whole trajectory of your day. Start small. Pay attention. Adjust as needed. Your rhythm is already there. You just have to find it.

AFTER 3–5 DAYS, LOOK FOR PATTERNS:

- When are your natural focus peaks?
- When do you consistently feel the urge to disengage or scroll?
- Is there a rebound period where your creativity wakes up again?
- What tasks drain you, even when you're energized?
- What tasks make you feel sharp—even when energy is lower?

PROMPT QUESTIONS TO REFLECT ON:

- What surprised you about your rhythm?
- How does your current schedule *support* or *sabotage* your energy?
- What's one small shift you could try next week?

Your body is giving you a productivity roadmap. This log just helps you read it.

WHEN YOU DON'T CONTROL YOUR CALENDAR

Let's be real—most of us don't have total autonomy over our workday. You might have a boss who loves 8:30 AM check-ins, or a calendar stacked with back-to-back meetings you didn't schedule and can't easily escape. Maybe your afternoons are chewed up by standing calls, or your creative windows are constantly interrupted.

That doesn't mean you're powerless.

Even when you can't overhaul your schedule, you can often influence the edges. Tiny shifts can create more space for your energy to breathe. Here are a few practical strategies you can try, even within a packed work structure:

1. ASK FOR TIME SHIFTS

If you notice your peak focus hits mid-morning but your most important meeting is at 9:00 AM, ask if it can be shifted to 10:00 AM next time. You'd be surprised how often people are flexible if you frame the request around being more present, thoughtful or prepared. Try: "Would it be possible to move this to 10:00 AM? I've found that's when I'm clearest and most focused."

2. BATCH SIMILAR TASKS

Group together admin-heavy or low-stakes tasks during your natural dips in energy (often mid-afternoon). This helps you save your sharper hours for deep work and decision-making.

Instead of writing reports and answering emails all day long, designate a 45-minute "shallow work" block where you knock those out in a sprint.

3. USE MINI-BREAKS FOR NERVOUS SYSTEM RESETS

Even a 5-minute walk, a short breathing exercise or simply staring out a window without your phone can reset your nervous system. You don't need an hour to get your clarity back. You just need to step out of go-mode for a few moments and let your brain reset.

4. BUILD BUFFERS AROUND SLUMP TIMES

If you always feel foggy around 2:30 PM, don't schedule important tasks then. Instead, drop in an easy task buffer—something repetitive or mechanical that won't require a ton of brainpower.

Filling out forms? Returning basic emails? Watching the annual compliance webinar? Perfect slump-time filler.

THE TAKEAWAY:

You may not control your entire calendar, but you *do* control more than you think. When you begin to design around your natural rhythms—even in small ways—you not only get more done, you protect your energy and sanity. And that makes you more powerful than any productivity hack ever could.

THE POWER OF MICRO-SHIFTS

You don't need to burn your calendar to the ground or quit your job to start honoring your natural rhythm. In fact, the most sustainable changes often begin as small, quiet experiments—micro-shifts that seem almost insignificant in the moment, but accumulate into meaningful transformation over time.

The truth is, your body's rhythm doesn't require a complete lifestyle overhaul to work with you. It just needs a few more moments of partnership instead of resistance.

Here are a few more micro-shifts you can try:

- **Protect one 90-minute block per week.**
  Just one. Block it on your calendar. Label it "strategy," "focus," or "creative flow." Use it for the kind of work that requires your best brain. Even this single pocket of protected time can make a measurable difference in your output and your confidence.

- **Insert 5-minute walking resets.**
  Between meetings, after deep focus, before launching into your email backlog—take five. Stand up, stretch, step outside, pace your space. Give your nervous system a window to exhale.

- **Shift one meeting time.**
  If there's a recurring meeting that cuts into your peak energy window, ask if it can shift—even by 30 minutes.

It doesn't have to be every meeting. Just one small win proves you can shape your schedule to serve your energy, not sabotage it.

- **Eat lunch without multitasking**.
  No laptop. No email. No scrolling. Just you, your food and your body's natural pause. Giving yourself that sliver of presence in the middle of the day creates space to reset and restore—without losing momentum.

Each of these shifts might seem small on paper. But over time, they send a powerful message to your brain and body: I'm listening. I'm adjusting. I trust the rhythm and I'm building a life that flows with it.

Because real change doesn't always arrive with fanfare. Sometimes it starts with a five minute walk and a quiet lunch.

REFLECTION ACTIVITY: IF YOU WERE BRAVE

This is your invitation to listen in—to pause long enough to tune into the natural ebb and flow of your day and then to make one small, brave decision in alignment with what you discover.

Grab a pen, your journal, or the notes app on your phone. Answer each question with honesty, not obligation.

1. **When do you feel most focused, clear, and alert?**
   Think about the times when your brain feels sharp and
   your work flows easily.
   This is likely your natural peak.

My natural peak time is:

_____

2. **When does your attention start to slip?**
   Consider when you tend to feel foggy, restless, hungry,
   or overwhelmed.
   This is your natural dip.

My focus usually fades around:

_____

3. **When do you feel most creative or open to new
   ideas?**
   Some people get a second wind late in the afternoon
   or evening. Others catch sparks of insight after move-
   ment or rest.
   This is your rebound zone.

My creative energy tends to arrive:

_____

4. If you were brave, what would you change to honor this rhythm?
Think small but meaningful. Would you block a focus window? Shift your email habits? Say no to one meeting? Take a real lunch break without your phone?

One brave shift I'd like to try is:

_____

OPTIONAL BONUS:

Write it on a sticky note. Post it where you'll see it. Remind yourself that this small act of alignment is not selfish—it's strategic. It's not indulgent—it's intelligent. And it just might change everything.

ENERGY IS YOUR COMPASS

You don't need to hustle harder. You don't need to cram more into the margins of your day. And you definitely don't need to keep measuring your worth by how exhausted you are.

What you need is alignment.

When you learn to recognize your own cycles—your peak hours, your natural dips, the moments your creativity hums— you begin to work *with* your energy, not against it. That's where momentum builds. That's where burnout recedes. That's where real, meaningful progress begins.

This chapter isn't about perfection. It's about permission. Permission to stop forcing yourself into systems that were never designed for human bodies. Permission to experiment.

Permission to trust that your body already knows what your brain is trying to figure out.

So take what you've learned here and begin, gently, to redesign your day.

Make one small shift. Honor one peak window.

Reclaim one stretch of time that belongs to your best self.

Because in the end? At the end of the day, energy—not time—is your most precious resource. And your rhythm? That's your roadmap. 🔑

CHAPTER FIFTEEN

Key: Your Gifts

IF THERE'S ONE through-line in this entire book, it's this: the more you understand yourself, the better your life starts to feel. Not perfect, not frictionless, but *real*. Aligned. Like something you actually chose—not something that happened to you.

That's why I believe self-awareness is the foundation of everything. Career satisfaction? Starts with knowing what energizes you. Healthy relationships? Starts with understanding your own patterns. Resilient leadership? Begins when you can see yourself clearly, strengths and shadows both.

And yet... most of us are walking around with only a partial picture of who we really are.

We're working from default settings, reacting to pressure, guessing at what might bring us joy. We say yes to things that drain us and no to things that might light us up—because we haven't taken the time to decode our own wiring.

That's where this chapter comes in. I want to help you get more precise. More curious. More empowered. Because when you understand your unique strengths—what comes naturally to you, what motivates you, how you best contribute—you gain a whole new set of tools to design a life that fits.

You don't need to be a different person. You just need to get really clear on who you already are. Let's start there.

WHY SELF-KNOWLEDGE CHANGES EVERYTHING

There's something powerful about having words for the things you've always *felt* but couldn't quite explain.

Maybe you've noticed you light up when you're brainstorming new ideas or that you feel drained after too much small talk. Maybe you've always been the one who spots potential in people—or who can walk into a chaotic situation and know exactly what to do. These traits feel obvious to you, so you might assume everyone has them. (Spoiler: they don't.)

That's the magic of self-assessment tools—not because they tell you something brand new, but because they help *name* what you've always sensed. They give shape to the gut-level instincts you couldn't quite articulate before. They offer a shared language for your inner world.

When you can clearly describe how you're wired, you stop second-guessing yourself. You stop trying to mimic other people's paths and start building your own. You make decisions faster. You recover from setbacks with more clarity. You begin to align your work, your relationships, even your calendar, around what actually works for *you*.

You don't need to fit a mold. You need to understand your own blueprint.

Because you can't build a life that fits until you know what you're made of.

ASSESSMENT TOOLS AND WHAT THEY OFFER

Over the years, I've taken just about every personality assessment out there—some insightful, some lighthearted and a few that were surprisingly accurate for a magazine quiz.

What I've learned is this: the right tool doesn't tell you who you are. It helps *reveal* who you are.

Here's a quick overview of some of the most commonly used tools and what they measure:

- **Myers-Briggs Type Indicator® (MBTI®)**
  Sorts you into a four-letter personality type based on preferences like introversion vs. extraversion, thinking vs. feeling, judging vs. perceiving. It's focused on how you perceive the world and make decisions.

- **DISC®**
  Maps how you respond to tasks, people and pressure. Are you Dominant (results-driven), Influential (people-oriented), Steady (supportive and reliable), or Conscientious (detail-focused)? It's often used in workplace settings to improve communication and collaboration.

- **Gallup's CliftonStrengths®
  (formerly StrengthsFinder®)**
  Focuses on your natural talents—patterns of thinking, feeling and behaving that come easily to you. It's based in positive psychology and emphasizes building on what's *right* with you. The CliftonStrengths® assessment measures the presence of talent in 34 areas called themes. Here's the really cool part -- a person's Top 5 Signature Themes are unique to the individual: 278,256 combinations of five themes are possible, and when you consider the specific order of the five themes, that number jumps to more than 33 million different combinations, meaning the likelihood of finding two people with the same Top 5 are one in 33 million. So your results truly are personalized and unique to you.

- **Enneagram**
  Digs into your *why*—your core motivation, fear and worldview. With nine basic types and countless nuanced variations, it's a powerful tool for personal growth and

emotional awareness. Enneagram's assessment results also depict what your personality type gets into conflict by being, which can change the conversation to focus on weakness.

- **Big Five (OCEAN)**
A collection of different assessments that measure personality across five dimensions: Openness, Conscientiousness, Extraversion, Agreeableness, and Neuroticism. Often used in psychological research.

- **Hogan, Birkman, Color Code, etc.**
Each has a specific lens—leadership potential, values alignment, interpersonal style—and can offer useful perspective in the right context. These traits help to understand individual differences in behavior, thoughts and feelings.

It's important to understand: *not all assessments are measuring the same thing*. Some focus on outward behavior, others on inner drives, some on conflict and disagreement, and still others on learned skills or natural wiring.

But across the board, the best assessments act as **mirrors**, not boxes. They're not there to confine you—they're there to reflect something essential you might not yet see clearly.

Something that, once named, becomes a tool for alignment.

DISCOVERING GALLUP'S CLIFTONSTRENGTHS® ASSESSMENT

The assessment that truly shifted how I saw myself—and how I built my work and life—was Gallup's CliftonStrengths®.

I first encountered it through the book *Now, Discover Your Strengths* by Don Clifton and Marcus Buckingham. The premise? Instead of focusing on what's broken and trying to fix it, what if we focused on what's *already right* with us and built from there?

That idea hit me hard.

So much of my career up to that point had been about trying to round out my edges—be less "extra," more detail-oriented, better at follow-through, more like someone else. But CliftonStrengths® flipped the script: What if those very quirks and instincts I kept trying to fix were actually the key to my success?

The science behind the tool is grounded in positive psychology. Gallup defines a *strength* as a natural talent that has been refined through awareness and practice. It's a pattern of thought, feeling or behavior that comes easily to you and, when used intentionally, produces near-perfect results.

Dr. Don Clifton's foundational belief was simple but revolutionary: **You grow most where you are already strong.**

Let that sink in.

In a world obsessed with improvement plans, performance gaps and 360 reviews pointing out what's "missing," CliftonStrengths® invites a radical reframe. It says: You're not a project to fix. You're a person with built-in brilliance—and your best path forward is to know it, trust it and use it on purpose.

That's what this tool gave me. Not just self-awareness, but *permission*. Permission to stop trying to be good at everything. Permission to double down on what already works. Permission to build a life that plays to my wiring instead of fighting against it.

And once I saw it that way, there was no going back.

MEET MY TOP 5 STRENGTHS

When I first received my CliftonStrengths® results, something clicked. Seeing those five themes together didn't just feel accurate—it felt like someone had handed me a map. A mirror. A permission slip. Suddenly, I had words for why I was the way I was—and better yet, how to use that wiring more intentionally. I want to share the results so that you can see how they rang true for me.

MAXIMIZER®

"Good enough" has never felt good enough to me. I've always had an eye for how to take something from solid to spectacular. Whether it's a presentation, a team dynamic or even how a dinner party flows, I instinctively spot opportunities for betterment. For years, I worried that made me too intense or picky. But when I saw Maximizer® as my top strength, it reframed everything. This isn't about being a perfectionist— it's about being tuned into excellence. Now, I consciously choose where to apply that energy. Not everything needs to be optimized. But when it *does* matter? I'm all in.

SIGNIFICANCE®

I've never been motivated by checking boxes. I want what I do to *mean* something—to ripple outward and create real impact. That drive for meaningful work has shaped every career decision I've made, from corporate roles to launching my own business and now to writing this book. Significance® explains why I light up when I'm coaching, teaching or mentoring. It's not about attention—it's about legacy. That theme helps me stay focused on what truly matters, not just what looks good on paper.

COMMUNICATION®

Words are my favorite tools. I love finding just the right analogy, turning a complex concept into something simple and sticky, or crafting a story that moves people. When I learned that Communication® was one of my top five, it helped me own that love of language instead of brushing it off as "just a quirk." Now, I use it on purpose—in my workshops, my writing and even in conversations that matter. It's one of the ways I connect most deeply with others.

LEARNER®

At any given time, I have about fifty different tabs open in my brain—books I'm reading, ideas I'm researching, new things I want to try. I used to get frustrated that I didn't always finish what I started, but CliftonStrengths® helped me see that curiosity itself is a strength. It keeps me on the leading edge. I now design my work around that desire to grow and explore. I give myself space to experiment, even if that means I don't always tie everything up with a bow.

FUTURISTIC®

If you hand me a blank page and ask me to imagine the future, I'm in heaven. I love thinking long-term, dreaming in high definition, setting goals and creating strategies to get there. I've been that way since middle school (I still have the notebooks to prove it). This strength shows up anytime I'm vision-casting—whether I'm helping a client imagine their next chapter, or planning a new business idea. Futuristic® fuels my hope. It reminds me that what's ahead can be even better than what's behind.

Together, these five themes feel like the most accurate self-portrait I've ever received. They explain how I operate, what I bring to the table and where I'm most likely to thrive. They help me understand how to design my life *on purpose*.

WHY THIS ONE FELT DIFFERENT

I've taken nearly every personality assessment out there—some out of curiosity, others as part of leadership development programs. Most gave me *something* valuable. But none of them had quite the same impact as CliftonStrengths®. Here's why.

MBTI® said that I'm an ENTJ, labeled the "Commander." Sure, the strategic thinking and goal orientation rang true. But the term *Commander* always felt a bit too cold, too confrontational for how I actually move through the world. I lead, yes—but I lead with connection, not just decisiveness.

DISC® identified me as a high "I"—the Influencer. That one made more sense. It explained why I love engaging people, building energy in a room and creating connection through conversation. But it still felt like a slice of the pie—not the whole thing.

The Enneagram typed me as a 3w4: The Achiever with a deep well of emotion and introspection. Again, some elements felt like me, such as providing language for my inner world, but it also wanted to highlight tension that I don't necessarily feel.

But **CliftonStrengths®**? That one gave me the *tools*. Not just a description of who I am, but a strategy for how to operate with alignment. It didn't just name my wiring—it showed me how to use it. The insight was practical, not just poetic. I could see how each theme showed up in meetings, in decisions, in team dynamics, in how I planned my day.

CliftonStrengths® helped me understand what energizes me and why. It offered a framework that's just as relevant in a coaching session as it is in a boardroom. And it gave me permission to stop chasing well-roundedness—and instead start focusing on becoming *well anchored* in who I already am.

That was the shift. Not just being *understood*, but being *equipped*.

REFLECTION ACTIVITY: KNOW THYSELF

Use the prompts below to explore how your natural wiring shows up in your life and where you might want to make small, brave shifts to align more fully with your strengths.

1. WHAT DO YOU ALREADY KNOW TO BE TRUE ABOUT YOURSELF?

Think about patterns you've seen your whole life.

- What are you naturally good at?
- What do people often come to you for?
- What gives you energy, even when you're tired?

2. HAVE YOU TAKEN ANY PERSONALITY OR STRENGTHS ASSESSMENTS BEFORE?

List any tools you've tried—MBTI®, Enneagram, DISC®, CliftonStrengths®, etc.

- Which results resonated with you?
- Were there any that didn't quite land?

3. WHAT ARE YOUR TOP 5 CLIFTONSTRENGTHS® (IF YOU KNOW THEM)?

Write them down.

- For each one, jot how you see it showing up in your day-to-day life.
- If you haven't taken the assessment, reflect instead on 5 things you believe are true about how you operate at your best.

Scan this QR code if you'd like to discover your CliftonStrengths® Top 5.

4. WHERE IN YOUR LIFE OR WORK DO YOU FEEL MOST ALIGNED?

- Where do you lose track of time, feel most energized or get consistent positive feedback?
- What are you doing in those moments—and who are you doing it with?

5. WHERE DO YOU FEEL DISCONNECTED OR OUT OF SYNC?

- Where do you feel like you're pushing uphill, overthinking or drained?
- Are there responsibilities, environments or relationships that don't play to your strengths?

6. IF YOU WERE BRAVE, WHAT'S ONE SHIFT YOU COULD MAKE TO WORK MORE WITH YOUR STRENGTHS INSTEAD OF AGAINST THEM?

Think small but meaningful.

- Could you delegate something, request a different kind of project or carve out time to do more of what lights you up?

BONUS: HOW DO YOUR STRENGTHS SHOW UP IN DAILY LIFE?

Choose one strength or trait and track it for a week.

- How does it help you problem-solve, connect, lead or create?

- What would change if you used it even more intentionally?

Remember: You don't need to be everything. You just need to fully be *you*. The more you know your wiring, the more clearly you can build a life that fits.

IT'S NOT ABOUT LABELS—IT'S ABOUT LEVERAGE

One of the biggest misconceptions about personality and strengths assessments is that they're meant to slap a label on you and call it a day. As if once you're typed—"You're a 3w4" or "You're an ENTJ"—you've been sorted into a box and handed a script. But that's not the point. Not at all.

The real power of these tools isn't in categorizing you. It's in giving you *language*—the kind that helps you articulate your instincts, advocate for your needs and work in a way that actually works for you. They offer insight you can use. Which means they're not about identity—they're about *leverage*.

Knowing your strengths or patterns can help you set healthier boundaries. For example, if you know that your energy thrives in deep work and tanks in constant interruptions, you can start protecting time in your schedule to support that. That's not being picky. That's being smart about how you're wired.

It also helps you say yes to the right projects—and no to the wrong ones. You can spot early when something's likely to energize you or deplete you. And you'll begin making more aligned choices on purpose, instead of out of habit or guilt.

Delegation gets easier, too. When you understand what you're *great* at, you stop trying to muscle through the things that drain you. You let go of the myth that you should be able to do it all. Instead, you find collaborators who shine where you don't—and you create a system where everyone thrives.

And if you're leading others? This self-knowledge becomes a superpower. Because when you know how *you* operate, you stop expecting everyone else to think, decide or respond the same way. You lead with clarity and compassion. You invite strengths instead of demanding sameness.

So no, it's not about putting yourself in a box. It's about unlocking the lid and realizing: *Oh, this is how I work best.* And now that I know that? I can use it. I can build around it. I can lead, live and create with more intention than ever before.

STRENGTHS AND RELATIONSHIPS

One of the most overlooked benefits of knowing your strengths is how it transforms your relationships. Whether you're part of a team, leading a group, parenting, partnering or collaborating with others—strengths give you a lens to see both yourself and those around you with more clarity and grace.

Every strength has a shadow and every strength has a complement. A big-picture visionary may need someone who thrives on detail. A fast mover might need a steady presence who asks thoughtful questions. A relationship-builder can thrive alongside a results-driven doer—if they recognize the value in one another's approach.

One of the most productive partnerships I've had was with someone whose CliftonStrengths® were almost the exact opposite of mine. Where I led with *Futuristic*® and *Maximizer*®—constantly scanning the horizon and refining ideas—she brought *Responsibility*® and *Consistency*®. While I was dreaming up version 4.0, she was building the scaffolding for version 1.0 to actually launch. Together, we moved things forward faster and better than either of us could have alone.

But here's the key: we *named* those strengths. We talked about them. We understood that what sometimes felt like friction ("Why are you slowing this down?" "Why are you rushing ahead?") wasn't a problem—it was a strength at work. It helped us pause, clarify and meet in the middle.

When you begin noticing the strengths of people around you, you stop assuming your way is the only—or best—way. You start to see what others bring to the table. You collaborate better. You offer empathy more easily. You let people be themselves while still working toward something shared.

And you create partnerships where strengths stretch and support each other in all the right ways.

BONUS WORKSHEET:
STRENGTHS SUPPORT SQUAD

Use this page to identify the people in your life whose strengths complement yours—and how that dynamic plays out.

Name	Their Strength or Style	How They Complement Me	How We Stretch Each Other

REFLECTION PROMPTS:

- Who helps you see things you might miss?
- Who balances your blind spots?
- Who energizes you with a different approach?
- What could you learn by leaning into those differences more intentionally?

This is your support squad. Let their strengths sharpen yours—and let yours do the same for them.

WHAT TO DO WITH THIS INSIGHT

Knowing your strengths is powerful—but only if you *do* something with that insight. Too often, we take assessments, nod in recognition and then tuck the results away in a drawer. But strengths are meant to be lived. Activated. Applied. Here are a few ways to start using your strengths with intention:

1. BUILD YOUR CALENDAR AROUND YOUR STRENGTHS.

If your strengths include *Focus*® or *Achiever*®, try time-blocking your day to match your drive. If you lead with *Relator*® or *Harmony*®, build in time for connection or relationship-focused tasks. Use your natural rhythm to fuel your productivity instead of fighting it.

2. REFRAME TASKS TO FIT YOUR WIRING.

Not every task is thrilling—but many can be approached through the lens of your strengths. Hate writing reports but love storytelling (*Communication*®)? Frame it as telling the story of what happened. Struggle with cold outreach but thrive on service (*Empathy*® or *Developer*®)? Approach the task as offering support instead of selling.

3. SHARE YOUR THEMES WITH YOUR TEAM OR PARTNER.

Knowing each other's strengths can shift everything in a working relationship or marriage. When you can say, "This is something I'm great at—and this is something that drains me," you open the door to deeper collaboration, less friction and more mutual respect.

4. USE YOUR STRENGTHS TO MAKE DECISIONS.

When you're weighing an opportunity, ask: Will this let me use what I do best? Will it energize me or drain me? Will it help me grow in alignment with who I really am?

5. START SMALL, BUT START.

Pick one of your top themes. Ask yourself how it showed up yesterday. Where it helped. Where it got in your way. Then make one micro-adjustment to lean into it even more today.

Because at the end of the day, your strengths are not just descriptive. They're directional. They point you toward the kind of work, relationships and life where you don't just survive—you thrive.

FINAL REFLECTION: IF YOU WERE FULLY ALIGNED WITH YOUR STRENGTHS...

Take a moment to imagine what your life might look like if your strengths weren't just something you *knew*—they were something you *used*.

If your day-to-day tasks matched the way your brain is wired.

If your calendar reflected your energy, not just your obligations.

If your goals were shaped by what lights you up—not just what you think you *should* be doing.

Ask yourself:

- What would shift in how I spend my time?
- What kind of work would I say yes to? What might I finally say no to?
- How would I approach collaboration, leadership or even rest differently?
- What would I build, launch or try—if I trusted that my strengths were enough?

Visualize one day—just one—designed around your natural wiring.

- *What happens in the morning?*
- *Who are you working with?*
- *What are you creating, solving, contributing?*
- *How does your body feel by the end of it?*

That version of your day? That version of you? It's not a fantasy. It's a blueprint.

That strength you've always had? The one people comment on or thank you for? The skill that feels easy but seems hard for others? It's not random. It's a breadcrumb. And when you follow those breadcrumbs, they lead you toward alignment—toward a life where your energy is well spent, your gifts are fully used and your days feel more like your own.

You don't need more hustle. You don't need a personality transplant. You already have what you need.

You don't need a new version of yourself. You need the clearest version. And now, you're getting closer. ⚷

CHAPTER SIXTEEN

Key: Boundaries

LET'S START WITH the truth—your worth isn't your job title. It isn't your salary. It isn't your house, the car you drive, the designer label on your purse or how well you keep the peace. Your worth isn't found in how many people you please, how agreeable you are or how few needs you express. You are worthy because you exist. Full stop.

You have gifts the world needs. Yes, you. Not once you lose weight, not once you land the perfect role, not once you finish your degree or another certification, not once you're less tired or more accomplished—now. Just as you are.

But here's what happens: when we lose sight of our inherent worth, we start outsourcing it. We look for proof in how much we're producing, how well we're performing, how little we're complaining. We put up with things that don't feel right. We let people talk over us, take from us, treat us like we don't get a say—because somewhere deep down, we've started believing we don't.

That's where boundaries come in. They're not about shutting people out. They're about telling the truth about what you need, what matters to you and what's no longer okay.

Boundaries are how we reclaim our space in the world.

And let's be honest: sometimes the situation really is unfair. Sometimes the other person really is asking too much. Sometimes it's *them,* not you. But sometimes? Sometimes it *is* you—letting your own needs fall to the bottom of the list, staying silent when you know better, shrinking to keep the peace. Learning to tell the difference is part of the work.

Because this isn't about blame. It's about ownership. It's about stepping into your life like you belong there.

You do.

WHY BOUNDARIES MATTER

For a long time, the word "boundaries" made me nervous. It sounded confrontational. Final. Like something you throw down in anger when you've had enough. But here's what I've come to learn: boundaries aren't walls. They're windows. They let in what nourishes you and block what depletes you.

Boundaries are not about rejection or punishment— they are about *preservation*. They protect your energy. They uphold your self-respect. They help you live in alignment with who you are and what you value. Without them, you're at the mercy of everyone else's needs, moods and opinions. With them, you get to live a life that feels like your own.

Dr. Henry Cloud, one of the most trusted voices in this area, says that boundaries define where you end and someone else begins. That distinction is everything. When you know where your responsibility ends, you stop over-functioning for others. You stop confusing compassion with compliance. You start making decisions based on what's true for *you*—not what keeps everyone else happy.

Think of boundaries as tools of clarity and care. They say, "This is what I need in order to show up well." They create the conditions where respect, trust and mutual understanding can thrive. And when used early—before things get out of hand—they prevent resentment from building up in the first place.

This chapter isn't about becoming combative or cold. It's about becoming clear. It's about learning to tell the truth— kindly and consistently—about what's okay for you and what's not. Because when you're clear, other people can adjust. But when you stay silent, they don't even know there's a line.

OLD STORIES, NEW VOICES

I was raised to be a "good girl." Quiet. Agreeable. Easy to be around. I learned early that making waves didn't end well and that disagreement—even when it lived loud in my chest—was best swallowed whole. My job, I believed, was to make others comfortable. Even at the cost of myself.

So I became a people pleaser. I didn't challenge opinions. I stayed small. I offered a polite "hmm" instead of my honest thoughts. I didn't see my mom ever speak up when she disagreed with someone and my dad's explosive temper made it clear that dissent wasn't welcome. The message was loud and clear: go along to get along.

Then I got a boss who shattered all of that.

He was sharp, fast and intimidating. A PhD with the ego to match and a mind that always seemed five steps ahead of mine. One day, he asked for my take on something and I defaulted to my old script: "I'm not sure." He stopped what he was doing, looked straight at me, and said, "If you don't have a point of view, you are useless to me."

It landed like a slap. Harsh? Absolutely. But also—true. That moment stopped me cold.

He wasn't saying I had to be perfect or have every answer. He was saying I needed to *show up*.

Use my voice. Have an opinion. Contribute.

And I realized... I didn't know how.

Disagreeing had always felt dangerous. Having a voice felt risky. I thought I had to be fully informed, polished and persuasive to say anything that might push back. I thought speaking up would make me unlikeable. And like so many girls raised in the era of "be nice, be pretty, don't cause trouble," I confused kindness with silence.

Research confirms this: girls are often praised for being pleasant and penalized for being assertive. We're taught that our value lies in being agreeable—not honest. But niceness without authenticity isn't kindness. It's self-erasure.

That moment with my boss was a turning point. It didn't happen all at once, but it planted the seed. I started learning what it meant to have a point of view—and to trust that it mattered. I still catch myself with the urge to hold back sometimes. But now, I know that shrinking doesn't serve me—or the people around me.

Using your voice takes practice. So does unlearning the old rules. But I promise you: the world doesn't need more agreeable women. It needs more honest ones.

TWO FRIENDS, TWO MASTERCLASSES

I've been lucky to witness what boundary-setting looks like when done with clarity, grace and a little bit of backbone. Two friends in particular showed me what it means to protect your peace without burning bridges—and each did it in a way that left me both awed and inspired.

The first is a social butterfly in the truest sense of the word. She's magnetic, warm and somehow manages to make everyone in the room feel like the most interesting person there. We worked together years ago and I've always admired how she moved through the world—effortlessly connecting with others, always open, always kind.

One day at work, someone approached both of us and said, "Hey, want to hear a joke?" My default response, rooted in my people-pleasing past, was "Sure," even though I had a sinking feeling about where it might go. Over the years, I'd learned that "jokes" from certain people were often code for something off-color, uncomfortable or outright offensive. I can't count the number of times I found myself frozen in place, caught between a forced chuckle and quiet shame.

But not her.

Without missing a beat, she smiled and said warmly, "Absolutely—as long as it doesn't involve race or hurt someone's feelings."

That moment has stayed with me for years. It was firm but not harsh. Clear without being confrontational. She didn't wait to be offended—she set the terms *before* anything even happened. It was a boundary, delivered with kindness and it changed the energy immediately. No one stomped away. No drama followed. She modeled how to take care of yourself *and* still care for the room.

The second masterclass came from a friend who was drowning in invitations. She's a fantastic realtor with a huge network of friends—many of whom, at some point, joined a homebased sales company. Candles, kitchen gadgets, skincare, essential oils—you name it. The invites kept coming: parties, pop-ups, group texts, last-minute sales goals. At first, she said yes to everything out of loyalty and love. But over time, she felt stretched thin, both financially and emotionally. Her calendar was packed and her peace was fraying.

Then one day, she did something brilliant.

She sent a kind, straightforward email to her entire circle. It went something like this: *"I love you. I love spending time with you. But I'm overwhelmed with party invitations and I need to protect my time. I won't be attending any more product parties. Please don't be offended if I decline—let's get lunch or catch up another way instead."*

Simple. Honest. Unapologetic. And incredibly freeing.

I remember reading her email and thinking, *You can do that?* You can just say no to something that doesn't work for you—even if it's wrapped in friendship or guilt or social pressure?

Turns out, you absolutely can.

Both of these women reminded me that boundaries don't have to be dramatic or defensive. They can be proactive. Thoughtful. Even gentle. And perhaps most importantly— they can be expressed *before* resentment builds. You don't have to wait until you're seething or exhausted or two steps from snapping.

You can simply say, "Here's what works for me."

And then stand in it. Not with armor, but with confidence. The kind that comes from knowing you're allowed to take up space, protect your energy and choose what you participate in.

And you know what? The world didn't fall apart. No one imploded. The sky didn't crack open. The people who mattered respected it—and the ones who didn't? Well, that's good information too.

Boundaries, when set early and kindly, don't just protect your peace. They set a tone. They invite others into healthier, more honest relationships. And they remind us that saying *yes* to ourselves isn't selfish—it's necessary.

WHEN IT'S ALREADY MESSY

Sometimes, you don't get the luxury of setting boundaries ahead of time. You walk into a situation thinking it's just lunch with family or a catch-up with an old friend and suddenly you're knee-deep in a political rant, a conspiracy theory or a monologue that makes your blood pressure rise.

If you're like I used to be, your default response might be to freeze, mumble something noncommittal and pray the topic changes. For a long time, I'd just nod or offer a quiet "hmm" because I didn't want to argue, didn't want to cause a scene and definitely didn't want to open the door to an hours-long debate. I thought I was keeping the peace.

But here's the catch: silence gets interpreted as agreement.

Before I knew it, these conversations weren't just happening—they were happening *more often*. And with more intensity. Why? Because I had unknowingly signaled that I was a safe space for those views. That I was on the same page. That I agreed.

And I absolutely did not.

So I had to start doing something different. Not arguing. Not lecturing. Just gently, clearly shifting the tone.

Here's what worked for me—short phrases that set a boundary without blowing things up:

- "That sounds like something you care a lot about. I don't find those conversations helpful so let's talk about _____ instead."

- "I've heard that, too—and I've also seen it fact-checked and found something different. How do you usually verify your sources?"
- "I love spending time with you, but I'm not interested in discussing politics. I'd rather talk about something lighter. Didn't you mention that you ran into Cousin Jim at Costco last week? How's he doing?"

The key here is brevity. You don't have to defend your values like you're on trial. You don't need to educate someone or change their mind. In fact, you likely *won't*. What you're doing is drawing a line: *This topic is off-limits with me.*

That's it. No explanation necessary. No apology required.

And if they keep pushing?

You bump up the boundary.

"Remember, I said I'm not comfortable having this conversation. If we can't move on, I'm going to have to cut this short."

That's not rudeness. That's clarity. That's self-respect. That's peace.

One of the most powerful things I've learned is that having a few mini-scripts ready in your back pocket makes it *so* much easier to speak up in the moment. You don't have to fumble or panic. You just reach for your line, say it calmly and shift the conversation.

It's not about winning. It's about choosing what you allow into your space. And once you start doing that with confidence, people notice. Not everyone will like it—but the ones who respect you? They'll adjust.

SCRIPT BANK – BOUNDARY PHRASES
FOR REAL LIFE

One of the most helpful things you can do when practicing boundaries is to have a few go-to phrases ready to use. When you're caught off guard or feeling pressured, a rehearsed line gives your nervous system something solid to stand on. You don't have to overthink it. You don't have to explain. You just say what's true.

Here's a list of real-life boundary phrases you can use in a variety of situations:

- "That doesn't work for me."
- "Let me think about that and get back to you."
- "I'm not taking on anything extra right now."
- "No, thank you."
- "That's not something I discuss."
- "I won't be able to make it."
- "That's not my story to tell."
- "Let's change the subject."
- "I'm not available for that."
- "I've made it a point not to talk about politics or religion."
- "That's not something I find helpful or appropriate."

Tip: Keep it short. Clear is kind—and saying less actually makes your message stronger. When you start justifying, over explaining or softening too much, you open the door to negotiation. Boundaries aren't about debate. They're about clarity.

A reminder for your back pocket: You don't owe any-one a lengthy explanation for protecting your time, peace or well-being. "No" is a complete sentence. And the more you practice saying it, the easier it becomes to mean it.

WHAT IF THEY IGNORE YOUR BOUNDARY?

Let's be honest—sometimes people don't respond well to boundaries. Especially if they've benefited from your lack of one for a long time. But here's the truth: **boundaries aren't about making someone behave differently. They're about deciding what you'll do when they don't.** That's where your power lives.

When someone crosses a boundary, you don't have to blow up. You don't have to explain yourself into exhaustion. You just escalate the clarity, not the volume. Here's how that can look:

LEVEL 1: REMINDER
Start with a calm, clear reminder.
- *"Hey, just a quick reminder—I'm not discussing politics these days."*
- *"Remember, I've stepped back from volunteering this season."*

LEVEL 2: REDIRECT

If they keep going, shift the conversation.

- *"Let's talk about something else—how's your garden doing?"*
- *"I'd rather not go down that road. What have you been reading lately?"*

LEVEL 3: CONSEQUENCE

If they still ignore your boundary, it's time to act—not react.

- *"If we can't change the topic, I'm going to step away for now."*
- *"This conversation isn't working for me. I'm going to end it here."*

You don't have to yell or justify. You don't have to make them understand or agree. Boundaries are not about controlling someone else. They're about honoring your own limits and being consistent in how you protect them.

You'll be amazed how much peace follows when you stop trying to convince someone to respect your boundary—and simply start living like it matters.

BURNOUT IN THE PARKING LOT

Melissa was a high-achieving marketing executive at a Fortune 50 company. On paper, she had it all—big title, big team, big results. But during a strengths discovery workshop I was leading for her group, I noticed something off. She radiated a kind of frenetic energy—tense, frantic, almost buzzing. The kind of energy that made my own nervous system feel jumpy just being near it.

After the session, I pulled her aside and gently asked if she'd be open to sharing what was really going on. She paused, then opened up.

"I get to the office no later than 7:00 AM," she said. "But it doesn't matter how early I show up—there are *always* people waiting in the parking lot to intercept me. Like, standing outside my car, ready to pounce."

My pulse picked up just imagining it. Ugh—people actually waiting in the parking lot?

"How does that feel?" I asked.

Her shoulders slumped. "Like I've already lost the day before it begins. I haven't even put my purse down and people are already asking for things."

It was heartbreaking. And familiar.

I asked her what an *ideal* day might look like. At first, she looked startled by the question.

Then she answered carefully, like testing out a fantasy she wasn't sure she was allowed to have.

"I'd wake up around 7," she said—though she phrased it like a question, like she needed my approval. "I'd drop off the kids, drive in and get to the office around 8:45. I'd be able to gather my things in peace, walk to my desk, set down my purse, grab a cup of coffee. Just... *arrive*."

I nodded. "Okay, what happens next?"

"I'd spend the first hour planning, getting grounded. Then I'd be ready to meet with the team. But I'd have that first bit of time to myself."

"Melissa," I said, "I don't think you need a fantasy. You need a boundary."

We talked about what she could say to her team. How to prep them for a change. How to communicate clearly, kindly and firmly. She agreed to try it: send a message, explain the new routine and ask for support. No drama, just direction.

What Melissa realized—what so many high performers forget—is that you're allowed to design your day. Even in corporate life. Even at the top. Especially at the top.

Sometimes you just need permission. Sometimes that permission has to come from you.

HOW TO PRACTICE HOLDING A BOUNDARY

Boundaries sound good in theory, but what does it look like to actually *hold one* in real life?

It starts with clarity. If you're changing a dynamic that's been in place for a while, give people a heads-up. Announce the shift with calm confidence, not defensiveness. A simple statement like, "Hey, I've realized I need to protect my mornings for focused work, so I won't be available for drop-ins until after 10 AM," can do a lot of heavy lifting. No need to overexplain—just share the new expectation.

Next, be specific and consistent. Vague boundaries confuse people. "I need more space" doesn't mean much. But "Please don't call me after 6 PM unless it's urgent" gives people something to work with. And once you set it, *stick to it*. If you waver at the first sign of pushback, you're training others to treat your boundary as optional. Remember, the goal isn't to avoid discomfort—it's to build alignment.

People may be surprised at first. That's okay. Give them time to adjust. Their initial reaction doesn't mean your boundary is wrong. It just means it's new.

Physical cues can help reinforce boundaries without a single word. Stand up when a conversation needs to end. Walk away from gossip. Close your laptop when the workday is done. Don't reply to the late-night text until morning. Hit pause on the group thread that's draining your energy.

The key is consistency. You teach people how to treat you by what you tolerate—and what you repeat.

As I often say to clients: *The psychic method doesn't work. Say what you need.*

PLATINUM RULE THINKING

We all grew up hearing the Golden Rule: *treat others the way you want to be treated*. It's well-meaning, sure. But over time, I've realized that it's incomplete. Because what works for you might not work for someone else.

You might love spontaneous drop-ins. I might need a heads-up and a calendar invite. You might recharge by being around people. I might need silence to reset. The way *you* want to be treated is valuable, but it's not universal.

That's where the **Platinum Rule** comes in: *treat others the way they want to be treated*.

To do that? You need to ask. And you need to tell.

That means stepping into conversations that clarify, rather than assuming you know what someone else needs—or silently hoping they'll just *get* what you need. Mutual respect starts with mutual understanding and you don't get there without communication.

So ask:

- "What's the best way for me to give you feedback?"
- "Do you prefer texts or emails for quick questions?"
- "What do you need from me in stressful weeks?"

And tell:

- "I need some quiet time before diving into decisions."
- "Mornings are when I focus best, so I won't be available for casual check-ins then."
- "I'd rather talk through feedback face to face than over Slack."

Setting boundaries and communicating preferences isn't rude. It's not defiant. It's not selfish.

It's actually the highest form of respect—because it says: *I care about this relationship enough to be clear. I care about you enough to ask what works for you. And I care about myself enough to be honest about what works for me.*

The more we practice this kind of clarity, the more trust we build—and the less room we leave for resentment, misunderstanding or burnout. The Platinum Rule creates space where both people can feel safe, seen and sovereign.

DEALING WITH PEOPLE WHO PUSH

Here's the hard truth: the people who have the hardest time with your boundaries are often the ones who benefitted most from your lack of them.

When you were always available, always agreeable, always accommodating—they got more of your time, your energy, your emotional labor. So when that changes, even if your boundary is kind and reasonable, it might feel like a loss to them. And some people? They don't like losing access.

They might test you. Push back. Guilt trip. Make it awkward. That doesn't mean you're doing it wrong. It just means your boundary is working.

And when those people start spiraling into unreasonable behavior—arguing every point, flipping your words, refusing to let it go—I want you to remember the best advice I ever got from our family counselor, Dr. Ray: *"You can't reason with unreasonable people. Stop trying."*

Seriously. You don't need to contort yourself into the perfect explanation, say it ten different ways or make it soft enough to be palatable to someone who was never going to accept it in the first place.

You don't owe anyone comfort at your own expense.

Boundaries are about protecting your peace, not managing someone else's reaction. The more consistently you practice, the clearer it becomes: people who care about you will learn to respect your boundaries. People who only cared about what you gave them may not.

Let that be clarifying—not crushing. Because once you start setting boundaries, you're not just protecting your energy. You're creating space for the right people to meet the real you.

REFLECTION ACTIVITY – BOUNDARIES

Take a moment to reflect honestly. You don't have to overthink or censor—just jot down what comes up for you.

1. **Where in your life would a boundary help?** (Is there a relationship, responsibility or recurring situation where you feel drained, overwhelmed or resentful?)

2. What are you tolerating out of fear or habit?

(What do you keep saying yes to even though your body says no? What's the story you tell yourself about why you "have to"?)

3. What would it feel like to say no?

(Get specific: Would you feel guilty? Relieved? Nervous? Empowered? Practice letting all those feelings exist.)

NOW TRY THIS FILL-IN-THE-BLANK BOUNDARY SCRIPT:

"Next time _____,
I will_____."
Example: "Next time my coworker dumps last-minute tasks on me, I will say I can't take anything new until tomorrow."

"If it continues, I will_____."
Example: "If it continues, I will speak with my manager about a better task distribution."

CHOOSE TWO POCKET PHRASES TO HAVE READY:

Phrase 1: _____
Example: "That doesn't work for me."

Phrase 2: _____

Example: "Let me get back to you."

These aren't just words—they're anchors. Use them to ground yourself when the moment arises. You deserve to take up space, preserve your peace and set the tone for what you will—and won't—carry.

BOUNDARIES ARE A FORM OF SELF-TRUST

Boundaries aren't walls to shut people out. They're doors you close gently, on purpose, to keep your peace intact. They're the way you tell yourself—and the world—where you end and where someone else begins. They are clarity. They are care. And most of all, they are trust.

When you set a boundary, you're not being dramatic, difficult or cold. You are protecting your energy, your time, your values and your well-being. You're not asking too much. You're asking for what's yours to protect.

And yes, some people won't like it. That's okay. You were never meant to shape-shift endlessly just to keep everyone comfortable. That's not your job. Your job is to be honest about what you need and brave enough to honor it.

Every time you hold a boundary, you remind yourself: *I matter here.* And that reminder?

It's worth everything. ⚷

CHAPTER SEVENTEEN

Your Aligned Life Starts Now

MOST MORNINGS, I begin my day with *The Daily Jay* on the Calm app. Jay Shetty's voice has a way of grounding me—equal parts thoughtful and gentle, like a friend reminding you what matters before the world comes rushing in. On one particular morning, he said something that stopped me mid-sip of Diet Coke. "When we identify with external factors," he explained, "we feel dissonance when those things change."

I sat there, heart suddenly heavier, because that was me. That *had* been me for a long time.

There was a time in my life when I measured my worth in job titles, salary bands, LinkedIn endorsements and the kind of handbag I carried into the quarterly meeting. I found validation in my frequent flyer status and felt oddly proud of how many hotel concierges knew me by name. I once saw these things as proof that I was doing it right. That I was winning.

Have you ever seen the movie *Up in the Air*? There's a scene where George Clooney and Vera Farmiga are sitting in a hotel bar, pulling out their airline and hotel loyalty cards like poker chips, trying to outdo each other. They get increasingly excited until Clooney plays his final card: the American Airlines Concierge Key. Farmiga stares in awe and says, "Oh my god. I wasn't sure this even actually existed."

The scene is absurd—and yet I remember watching it and feeling *seen*. That was me.

That was the language I spoke. I once checked into a hotel in Boston, placed my status card on the counter like it was currency and beamed when the front desk associate looked at me in surprise. "Is this your card?" she asked. "I've just never seen someone so young achieve this level." I remember the pride that bloomed in my chest like it was yesterday. I felt ten feet tall.

But now I look back with different eyes.

How many flights did I take to earn that recognition? How many hours did I spend away from home, away from connection, away from myself? How many moments did I miss in the name of being "important" to a company that replaced me in less time than it took to use my hotel points?

How much of myself did I give away just to earn a better hotel room or earlier boarding group?

This chapter isn't about regret. It's about awakening.

Because what I've come to realize is this: when we anchor our identity in things that live outside of us—titles, perks, applause—we lose access to the compass inside of us. And when those external things shift or disappear (as they always do), we're left untethered, unsure of who we are without them.

But you are *not* your job title. You are not your business card, your income or your inbox. You are something far deeper, far truer.

And if you're ready to start building a life that reflects *that* version of you—the one that exists even when the title is gone—then you're in the right place.

Your aligned life starts now.

MY YOUNGER SELF

If I could sit down with my younger self—the version of me hustling through airports, glued to a BlackBerry, proudly stacking up status points like they meant something eternal—I wouldn't scold her. I wouldn't even try to fix her. I would simply look her in the eye and say, "You deserved more than this."

She was doing what she thought she was supposed to do. She was being responsible. Practical. Impressive, even. She said yes to every opportunity, chased every promotion and rarely paused long enough to ask, *Do I even like this?* She didn't take the photography class. She didn't join the club. She didn't skip the occasional meeting just to sit in the sunshine or laugh until her stomach hurt. Because that wasn't "the plan." That didn't check any boxes.

She believed that being taken seriously meant constantly proving she was useful. That rest was something you earned once you were exhausted. That success was measured by external approval, not internal peace.

But if I could speak to her now, I'd tell her to slow down. Try the silly thing. Go out with friends. Make a mistake. Don't pick the practical option *just because it's practical*. Not everything has to serve some arbitrary purpose to be worth doing.

I say this to my daughters nearly every time they walk out the door: *"Be young. Have fun. Make good choices."* And I mean every word. I want them to know that they don't have to earn their way into joy. That they are allowed to feel alive without proving anything. That life doesn't wait for some perfect mythical moment when everything is under control.

Looking back, I wish someone had said that to me. I wish I had said it to myself. But the beautiful thing is—I can say it now. And I can live it forward.

FULL CIRCLE MOMENTS

A few years after my own unraveling—and the rebuilding that followed—I found myself running a quick errand to pick up contacts from my optometrist's office. I wasn't thinking about work, certainly not about the past. I was in jeans and a hoodie, just out living life.

As I reached for the door, someone stepped out. We locked eyes for half a second, and I knew immediately who it was—someone I had once worked with. More than that, someone I had once had to let go.

Those moments are never easy. Even when it's done professionally, with compassion and dignity, it still feels like a rupture—for them and for the person delivering the news. I remembered the day vividly. I remembered the knot in my stomach. I remembered wanting to handle it as gracefully as possible, even though I knew how painful it would be.

He recognized me too. And to my surprise, his face broke into a big smile.

"Hey," he said warmly, "it's really good to see you."

We chatted for a moment, and then he said something I'll never forget.

"I want you to know—I'm actually grateful for how things ended. You handled it with so much grace. And honestly? It gave me the push I needed. I used the severance to start my own music school. It's going great. I've never been happier."

I stood there, blinking in the afternoon sun, humbled by the full-circle moment I hadn't seen coming.

Here was someone whose chapter had closed in a way I never wanted—but he turned the ending into a beginning. A better one. A truer one. An aligned one.

And I realized something that day: not every painful decision stays painful. Some of them rip something open that needed to be released. Some of them clear space for something we wouldn't have chosen—but desperately needed.

Even hard endings can become sacred turning points.

And sometimes, if we're lucky, we get to see the redemption unfold right in front of us.

YOU'VE BUILT YOUR TOOLKIT

Let's pause here for a moment and take a breath.

You've done something big—something rare. You've walked through chapter after chapter of reflection, courage, curiosity and clarity. You've asked better questions. You've told yourself the truth. You've started letting go of what doesn't work and reaching for what does.

And along the way, you've built a toolkit. Not someone else's version of success. Yours.

You now understand that **alignment is the key**—and misalignment shows up in your calendar, your energy, your body and your beliefs. You've learned how to notice it early, before the whisper becomes a shout.

You've started **reconnecting with your inner voice**, with the version of you who still remembers joy, creativity and possibility. You met your 9-year-old self again—the one who knew what she liked and wasn't afraid to say it.

You've mapped your life season and seen how different times call for different rhythms and expectations. You gave yourself permission to be in winter or spring or any season that called for rest or risk or rebuilding.

You've taken time to name the things that **bring you joy**, that energize you, that light up your nervous system in a way that feels like truth. And you've questioned the myth that joy is a luxury. You now understand: it's a compass.

You've explored the role of **personal engagement**—using Gallup's model to map where in your life you're fully engaged, just going through the motions, or actively drained. You used color (green/yellow/red) to track your patterns and made room for honesty. You learned that **energy is data**, not judgment.

You've looked at how your body is always speaking—and how **somatic signals** show up before your mind can explain what's wrong or right. You've mapped your physical responses to joy, stress, dread, flow and more. You've practiced tuning in instead of pushing through.

You've learned the **science of natural rhythms**—especially ultradian rhythms—and the power of aligning your work to your peak focus windows. You saw how productivity isn't about willpower. It's about flow, recovery and working with your biology, not against it.

You've taken a close look at your **strengths**, your wiring, your inner code. You learned how assessments like CliftonStrengths® can give you powerful language, not just to describe who you are, but to **build a life around it.**

You've started redefining **success on your terms**—away from external markers like job titles or status levels and toward something quieter, truer: peace, meaning, connection, joy, contribution.

You've looked at the role of **boundaries**—not as walls, but as clarity. You practiced short, strong phrases. You learned that you don't owe long explanations. That "no" is a full sentence. That protecting your time, energy and values is an act of **self-trust**, not selfishness.

You've acknowledged that **visualization isn't woo woo**—it's neuroscience. You practiced seeing, feeling and mentally rehearsing the aligned life you want to live. You mapped what you're moving toward, not just what you're leaving behind.

You learned to **spot early signs of misalignment**, to stop waiting for the hammer and listen for the feather. You reflected on the lessons from burnout, over-functioning, self abandonment—and you chose a new way.

You rewrote rules that were never yours to carry. You challenged old stories that said "this is just how it is." You asked instead: What if there's a better way? What if life could feel more like me?

You practiced **bravery in small steps**—blocking your mornings, saying no to an event, letting go of guilt, asking for what you need.

And most of all, you began to believe in yourself and in a life intentionally designed to fit you best.

You are already equipped. Already worthy. Already in motion. This toolkit isn't just a box of ideas. It's a living, breathing practice. And it's one you now carry with you—for whatever comes next.

REFLECTION ACTIVITY: ONE SMALL SHIFT

You don't need to flip your life upside down to begin living in alignment. In fact, most meaningful change begins quietly—with one brave decision, one boundary held, one honest conversation that opens the door to something better.

Use the prompts below to help you name the next right step—not the perfect step, not the final one, just the next one that feels honest, doable and aligned. Then commit to taking action on it within the next 72 hours. Because clarity without action just becomes clutter.

Take a deep breath. And then take five minutes to write:

1. ONE THING I'M CURRENTLY DOING THAT FEELS MISALIGNED:

This might be a habit, a commitment, a dynamic or even a belief. What's draining you, distracting you or pulling you out of alignment?

2. ONE SMALL CHANGE I COULD MAKE THIS WEEK:

What would feel like a course correction? What's one shift—however small—that would move you closer to what matters?

3. ONE BOUNDARY I'M READY TO HOLD:

Where do you need a line? What have you been tolerating or over functioning around a boundary that needs a clear, kind "no more"?

4. ONE CONVERSATION I'M READY TO HAVE:

Who do you need to talk to? What do you need to name? Don't script it perfectly. Just start. Say the thing.

YOUR 72-HOUR COMMITMENT:

Before this becomes just another powerful page you read and set aside—choose your action. Schedule it, speak it or write it down and share it with someone you trust. Then take that first step. Not because it will fix everything, but because it will remind you of this truth:

You're allowed to choose what fits. And you're strong enough to follow through.

A LIFE THAT FEELS LIKE YOURS

You don't have to torch your career, move to a mountaintop or reinvent yourself from scratch to live in alignment. This is not a dramatic before-and-after story. It's something gentler—and, in many ways, far more powerful.

Aligned living doesn't demand that you burn it all down. It simply asks you to notice. To choose. To practice. And then do it again.

It begins with small things: realizing you feel more alive when you work outdoors. Noticing that your body tenses around a certain person. Recognizing that your best ideas come not from grinding harder but from walking the dog or taking a hot shower. It's in those moments of self-awareness that you get to choose what to do differently—what to protect, what to stop, what to begin.

Living in alignment is not a destination you arrive at with trumpets and champagne. It's a path. A way of walking through life with more presence, more self-trust and more truth. Some days it will feel smooth and spacious. Other days, you'll forget everything you've learned here.

That's okay. You're not supposed to be perfect. You're just supposed to be honest.

What matters most is momentum—those repeated acts of self-respect that build over time into a life that feels like yours.

So drop the pressure. Release the fantasy of getting it "just right." Start where you are.

Choose what matters. Practice again tomorrow. And again the next day.

That's how alignment is built—not by force, but by faith. Not by perfection, but by presence.

YOU ARE NOT BEHIND

If there's a whisper in the back of your mind saying, *"I should've figured this out by now,"* I want you to know—you're not alone. So many people reach this point in the journey and start to question everything: *Is it too late to change? Have I gone too far in the wrong direction?*

WHY DIDN'T I START SOONER?

Alignment doesn't follow a calendar. There is no expiration date on growth, clarity or joy. There is only *now*. And right now is always a good time to begin again.

You haven't missed your moment. You haven't taken a wrong turn too far to return. You haven't wasted the years—it all brought you here, with hard-won insight and the exact perspective needed to make this next chapter the most intentional one yet.

Whatever your past has held and however long you've felt out of sync, know this: **You are not behind. You are not broken. You are not too much or too late. You are right on time.**

And from here, you get to choose what's next.

FINAL REFLECTION – YOUR ALIGNED LIFE

As you close this chapter—literally and metaphorically—take a moment to pause and take stock. This isn't just the end of a book. It's the beginning of a deeper relationship with yourself.
Ask yourself:

- **What does a fully aligned day look like for me?**
Picture it in detail. What time do you wake up? What kind of work are you doing? How do you feel in your body? Who's around you—or not? What's different about your energy, your presence, your pace?

- **What's something I want to stop measuring my worth by?**
Maybe it's your productivity. Your salary. Your title. Your weight. Your inbox count. Let it go. You're not a machine. You're a human being with inherent worth that does not fluctuate with performance.

- **What's one practice or habit that helps me stay aligned?**
Is it checking in with your body each morning? Protecting your peak energy window? Reviewing your strengths? Journaling? Moving your body? Speaking your truth, even when it's scary?

As you reflect, return to your notes from earlier chapters. Look for the themes, the patterns, the a-ha moments that stood out to you. The places where something clicked or stirred. That's your map. That's the outline of your aligned life already taking shape.

You don't need to have it all figured out. You just need to keep listening, adjusting and choosing what fits. Alignment is a practice—and you're already in it.

GO LIVE IT

Alignment isn't something you have to chase—it's something you already carry inside you. It's not a destination you arrive at when you finally check every box or prove every point. It's the quiet, steady knowing that's been with you all along. The pull toward what feels true. The whisper that says, *this is who you really are.*

You've done brave work in these pages. You've looked at what's working, what isn't and what you long for. You've mapped your rhythms, your strengths, your signals, your values. You've named the boundaries you're ready to hold, the beliefs you're ready to release and the life you're ready to build. You've gotten honest—and that's everything.

So now, the invitation is simple.

Go live it.

Not the perfect version. Not the curated version. The *true* one. The version where you say yes on purpose and no without apology. Where you move with your energy instead of against it. Where your work, your relationships and your day-to-day choices reflect the person you are—not the one you've been told to be.

Because you don't need a new version of yourself.

You need the clearest version.

You are worthy. You are wise. You are right on time. And your aligned life? It's waiting for you—not someday, but now.

Be brave. Be intentional. Be aligned.
Your life starts now.

⚷

ACKNOWLEDGMENTS

So many incredible people have played a part in bringing this book to life. First, my husband and soulmate, Tom, and our girls, Hansley and Halley. You are a master class in what truly matters, and I want you all to know that you are each worthy and enough. I am beyond grateful for your love, support and the lessons you teach me every day.

Thank you to my mom, whose trailblazing spirit and love of learning have shaped who I am today.

A special thank you to my friend of over 30 years and podcast co-host, Kyla Martin (Turn the Page: Design Your Dream Career with Kyla and TyAnn). All those emergency trips to Cabo were worth it—we are truly living the life we've imagined.

Many thanks to my friend and colleague, Lisa Cummings of Lead Through Strengths, and her Tools for Coaches community. Our favorite question to ask—What would we do if we were brave?—has inspired us to stretch beyond what we ever thought possible. Thanks to that, our lives and businesses have unfolded in ways we could have only dreamed about.

I owe a special shout-out to my colleague and friend, Charlotte Blair of The Strengths Partners, author of Career Unstuck, and my relentless cheerleader. It was because of her that I connected with Kelly Irving's Expert Author Community, where I found my book pod and fellow writers Jennifer Doyle Vancil, Siobhan O'Riordan, Monique Zytnik and Chloe Temple.

These women are world-class in every sense, offering endless patience and support.

To Miriam Rieck, author of *On Becoming* and virtual assistant extraordinaire—without you, none of this would exist. Your dedication and insight have been invaluable and I can't imagine my life without you.

To CJ Redwine, for transforming my ramblings and corralling my stories. To Sarah Lahay, for your mad skills in book layout and typesetting. And to the rest of the amazing members of Team Ty: Amy Martin, Yael Karoly, Will Taylor and Katie Mack. You've made work smoother and more enjoyable than I could have imagined.

Thank you to everyone who believed in me and my vision, and to those who walked alongside me every step of the way. This book is a reflection of all your support, encouragement and love.

With all my gratitude,
TyAnn

ABOUT THE AUTHOR

TyAnn is an executive coach, speaker, podcast co-host (Turn the Page: Design Your Dream Career) and Gallup-certified CliftonStrengths® expert dedicated to helping people live and work in greater alignment with who they truly are. Drawing on years of leadership experience in Fortune 100 companies and her work with tens of thousands of professionals, she guides others in reclaiming purpose, energy and fulfillment in every part of life.

Through her coaching, workshops and now her first book, *A Life Aligned: Keys to Transform Your Work and Life*, Ty offers practical tools and heartfelt encouragement to those who are ready to design a career—and a life—that truly fits.

When she's not coaching, speaking or writing, Ty enjoys hiking in Big Bend National Park and finding the best chicken-fried steak. She and her family live in Texas. Learn more at www.tyannosborn.com.